MY NAME iS TANI

...and I BELIEVE in *MIRACLES*

YOUNG READERS
EDITION

MY NAME IS TANI

...and I BELIEVE IN *MIRACLES*

YOUNG READERS
EDITION

BY TANI ADEWUMI

WITH CRAIG BORLASE

THOMAS NELSON
Since 1798

My Name Is Tani ... and I Believe in Miracles Young Readers Edition

Published in Nashville, Tennessee, by Tommy Nelson. Tommy Nelson is an imprint of Thomas Nelson. Thomas Nelson is a registered trademark of HarperCollins Christian Publishing, Inc. Tommy Nelson, PO Box 141000, Nashville, TN 37214.

Tommy Nelson titles may be purchased in bulk for educational, business, fund-raising, or sales promotional use. For information, please e-mail SpecialMarkets@ThomasNelson.com.

The names and identifying characteristics of certain individuals have been changed to protect their privacy.

ISBN 9781400218318 (eBook)
ISBN 9781400218295 (SC)
ISBN 9781400218325 (Audiobook)

Library of Congress Cataloging-in-Publication Data

Names: Adewumi, Tani, 2010- author. | Borlase, Craig, author.
Title: My name is Tani ... and I believe in miracles / by Tani Adewumi with Craig Borlase.
Description: Young readers edition. | Nashville, Tennessee : Thomas Nelson, [2020] | Includes bibliographical references. | Audience: Ages 8-12 | Audience: Grades 4-6 | Summary: "Tani Adewumi's powerful story of finding a new life in America will inspire young readers"-- Provided by publisher.
Identifiers: LCCN 2019052030 (print) | LCCN 2019052031 (ebook) | ISBN 9781400218295 (paperback) | ISBN 9781400218318 (epub)
Subjects: LCSH: Adewumi, Tani, 2010---Juvenile literature. | Chess players--United States--Biography--Juvenile literature. | Nigerian Americans--Biography--Juvenile literature. | Christian biography--Juvenile literature.
Classification: LCC GV1439.A34 A3 2020 (print) | LCC GV1439.A34 (ebook) | DDC 794.1092 [B]--dc23
LC record available at https://lccn.loc.gov/2019052030
LC ebook record available at https://lccn.loc.gov/2019052031

Printed in the United States of America

20 21 22 23 24   PC/LSCC   10 9 8 7 6 5 4 3 2 1

Mfr: LSCC / Crawfordsville, IN / March, 2020 / PO #9582652

CONTENTS

CONTENTS

CHAPTER 1

DO YOU BELIEVE IN MIRACLES?

Everything is gray and empty outside the bus depot. The sky looks like concrete and the concrete looks like the sky. Nobody else is around. It's just me, Mom, Dad, and my brother, Austin. Waiting. I'm wondering if someone has stolen the sun and all the people along with it.

I'm waiting beside the biggest pile of luggage I've ever seen. Most of our bags are way too heavy for me to lift, and some are so big I could fit inside. We need this much luggage because everything we own—Mom's frying pan, Dad's suits, my brother's books, and my toys—is packed away inside.

It's early in the morning. So early that the sky isn't even fully light yet. And that means it's *way* too early for Austin to talk. Mom and Dad are quiet too. Even

1

I'm not talking much, which is *really* unusual. I like asking questions, especially when I'm somewhere new. But right now, here in this empty old bus depot in Dallas, I don't feel like talking. It's like we've all run out of words.

Maybe it's because it's cold. When I breathe out, I can see my breath making little clouds in front of me. But they don't last. They just get swallowed up into the nothingness.

I stare at the bags. My stomach twists a little and a question grows inside of me. "Mom," I say. "You've still got my pilot pin?"

She smiles and taps the small bag that's on her shoulder. It's the one that has all our most important things, like passports and her phone and money. She knows how special my pin is to me. I want to be a pilot one day, maybe the youngest pilot *ever*. I've wanted this since I saw a real pilot interviewed on TV. He had saved a plane from crashing and was able to make sure all his passengers were safe. But I had never been on a plane until we flew from Nigeria, Africa, to America several months ago. And it was my first time ever seeing an actual pilot right there in front of me. I felt shy but he was really nice. And when we left the plane, he gave me a special pilot's pin that looked just like the one on his shirt. That was a good day.

We stand in silence awhile longer. There are empty benches all around us, but we don't sit. We don't want to sit. We want to go.

I'm bored. Dad is reading messages on his phone. Mom is looking out for the bus. Austin is trying to sleep standing up—which is impossible.

"What's it going to be like?" I ask him.

He opens an eye and looks at me like I'm from another planet. "What?"

"The next place. What's it going to be like?"

He sighs. "I don't know. Better than here, I guess."

I think about that for a while. "I hope so," I say. We've only been living here in Dallas for a few months, but I'm ready to leave.

A few more silent minutes go by. Dad's still reading. Mom's still checking. Austin's given up on trying to sleep. He's staring into the distance for the bus.

Another question appears inside me, and I have to ask it. "Austin," I say. "Where are we going to live?"

He shrugs and keeps staring out. "Dad knows."

I look back at Dad. He looks even more tired than the rest of us. I want to ask him, but before I can, Austin calls out, "At last!" and the air fills with the sound of an engine.

There's a sign in the bus window: "Destination: New York City."

Who Is an Immigrant?

An immigrant is a person who has come to live in a new country. People immigrate because they believe their lives will improve in a new place. Some people immigrate in search of better jobs, safer places to live, or better education for their children. Sometimes they are escaping a government that mistreats them or others who want to harm them because they are part of a certain religion or people group.

Dreams of a brighter tomorrow have been bringing people to America since the Pilgrims landed in 1620. Immigrants and their children founded the United States, farmed the land, started businesses, and passed down traditions from their homelands to the next generation. Over time, this mix of different cultures became the heart of America's identity.

Some of America's greatest citizens have been immigrants. Founding father Alexander Hamilton was born in the Caribbean. Inventor Nikola Tesla and mathematician Albert Einstein relocated to the United States. The father of the newspaper, Joseph Pulitzer, was an immigrant. Today, founders of Yahoo, Google, and YouTube are Americans born in other countries. As immigrants continue to contribute their skills, rich cultures, and new ideas to the nation, the United States moves closer to the better future we all hope for.

This bus ride is sooooo long. We drive by fields and forests and pass through cities with strange names I've never heard of. Dad told us it would take thirty-six hours to reach New York, but it feels like thirty-six days.

We stop at other bus stations from time to time. It's good to be able to move, but we never stay long. Soon the bus engine starts up again, and we have to get back to our seats. We squeeze past all the people sitting silent with their headphones on and return to our seats and the road and the fields and the forests and the road and the fields and the forests.

This is the second time we've been on this bus ride. Five months ago, we rode over these highways but in the other direction: from New York to Dallas. Everything was different then.

On the first bus ride, I was so excited. We had just landed in America, and every place I looked there was something that made me say, "Wow!" When you've spent your *whole life* living in Nigeria—even if it is in Abuja, the capital city—America is really different. The buildings are really tall. The lights are really bright. There are even giant video screens by the roadside telling you about things you can buy, like hamburgers and swimming pools and even ways to make your teeth look nice. I said a lot of *wows* on that first ride.

I'm not saying so many *wows* on this journey. In fact I'm not really saying any. I've seen lots of tall buildings, lots of bright lights, and lots of big screens selling things. And I've discovered that not everyone in America is as nice as I thought they would be.

Soon the sun sets and the sky turns dark again. The longer we drive, the darker it gets.

We stop again. Mom asks if I want to eat, but I don't see anything I like, so I just wait around for the engine to start up again. Then it's time to climb back into the bus and continue driving in the darkness. Soon there are no lights at all outside. There is only darkness.

Dad turns around and pushes his head through the gap in the seats in front of me. He's looking serious. "Are you well, Tanitoluwa? You are quiet today."

I like it when he uses my full name. The way he says *Tan-ee-tow-OO-ah*, fast and deep. It sounds like someone is beating on a drum.

"I'm fine," I say.

He frowns. "Are you nervous?"

Suddenly my stomach feels strange. It's like there's an elephant inside me, and it's making me feel uncomfortable. I always feel this way when I get nervous.

Dad gives me one of his smiles—the kind where his whole face goes big and wide and his eyes shine bright. "Listen to me carefully. We have been in America for five months now. It has not been what we thought. But today is a new start for our family. Wherever we are going, the Lord God goes with us."

I nod. Austin has taken off his headphones, and he's listening to Dad too.

"Let me ask you both a question," Dad says. "Do you believe in miracles?"

Austin and I both nod immediately.

"So do I. I believe in them because I have seen them with my own eyes. The way that God rescued us from Nigeria—that was a miracle. And the fact that we are here today, together on this bus—well, that is another miracle. So we are moving forward because God is with us and we are never alone. And whatever life holds for us in New York, I know that this one thing is true. We can expect God to be with us. And there will be more miracles as well."

I like it when Dad talks like this. He makes me feel strong and happy and like there's nothing to be scared of *ever*.

"Remember," he says, "wherever we go, we do not go alone."

I settle back into the soft seat. And as we drive deeper into the dark night, I remember the miracles that have brought us here.

CHAPTER 2

THE NIGERIAN PRINCE

I was six years old when we left Nigeria, so I don't remember much about the time we lived there. But I have some memories, like going to big family parties where all my cousins and uncles and aunts were laughing and talking and we ate the nicest food I've ever had in my entire life.

I've got to tell you that Nigerian food is the *best* food. We have really spicy stews and fried meats that smell delicious. We eat with our hands a lot of the time, and if you do it right, you can scoop up all the delicious broths using the pounded yam, which is a little like a ball of really thick mashed potatoes. It takes practice though; you have to twist your wrist and hold your fingers just right so the sauces don't drip everywhere and get super messy. It's a little easier to eat my favorite thing ever: jollof rice. Jollof rice is full of spices and tomatoes and peppers, and it makes your mouth feel awake and alive long after you've swallowed it.

In some ways, life in Nigeria wasn't that different from what yours is like. In Abuja, we had a nice house with a big, strong front door with heavy locks and a large TV in the living room. Austin and I shared a room, and we had bunk beds. Mom worked in a bank. Dad owned a big shop where people could get posters and books printed, and he drove a Toyota around the city, meeting with clients. Austin and I went to an English-speaking school. I liked playing on the computer and kicking a soccer ball in the yard with Austin and our friends.

There's another thing that I remember: a lot of people in Nigeria were worried. People were scared because these really bad people called Boko Haram decided that they wanted to kill Christians. I don't remember much more than that.

But I've learned enough about what happened to us to believe what Dad says: God rescued us. And it was a miracle.

I know something else as well. God didn't rescue us on His own; He used Dad.

And here's one more thing that I'm sure of: Dad is the bravest person I know.

What Is Boko Haram?

Boko Haram is an African terrorist group that believes in an extreme version of Islam. The group teaches that it's *haram* (which means "forbidden") to take part in anything to do with Western (American and European) culture. Boko Haram bans its followers from voting, going to non-Muslim schools, and even wearing Western clothes like shirts and pants. It also attacks people who do not follow those rules. The group often targets Christians and bombs churches. Since 2009, the group has killed about thirty thousand people and has caused two million Africans to leave their homes.

The group is most at work in Nigeria, especially the northeast of the country. There, in 2014, Boko Haram fighters carried out one of their most shocking crimes—capturing more than two hundred schoolgirls. Boko Haram leaders said that they would treat the girls as slaves and marry them off. Boko Haram has also been active in other parts of central Africa, including Chad, Niger, and Cameroon.

When members of Boko Haram visited Tani's dad's print shop, they wanted him to print a poster that said, "No to Western Education" and "Kill All Christians." When he did not agree to print it, Tani's dad became a target.

Dad is an actual prince. That's kind of amazing, right? An actual *prince*! His grandfather was a king in Nigeria. But Dad didn't grow up living in a palace or flying in private jets. In the part of Nigeria where we come from, kings don't have lots and lots of servants or sit around all day being lazy. They're also not born knowing they'll be kings. The people choose their king to do a special job: to help people, give wise advice, and make good decisions when people can't decide what to do.

Dad learned from his dad and his grandfather (the actual king!) to treat people well and to make good choices and to stand up for what he believes in. So even though Dad was not a king, people would often visit the house and tell Dad their problems and ask for his advice. Dad was always kind and patient with them and always did whatever he could to help.

But one day, Dad had some visitors at work who weren't so welcome.

They were part of Boko Haram. They wanted Dad to work for them. They wanted him to print a poster with a message of hate against Christians. But Dad refused. And when that happened, the men from Boko Haram got mad. Really mad.

Austin and I were asleep in bed one night, and Dad was out working. Mom was watching TV when she heard a knock on the door. She thought it was Dad forgetting his keys, so she opened it. Two angry men burst in. They searched the house, trying to find Dad's laptop, but they couldn't find it because Dad had it with him. They shouted and threw things around, and Mom was terrified. She was scared that the men from Boko Haram were going to hurt her or find Austin and me and do something bad to us. So she prayed.

And then they left.

That was the first miracle.

The men came back a few weeks later. Dad was home this time, and it was late at night again, so Austin and I were asleep. The men banged on the door and shouted for Dad to come out and hand himself over to them. Dad told Mom to go back to our bedroom, make sure we were okay, and pray.

Then he got on his knees and prayed too. As Dad prayed, the men yelled and beat on the door. "We know you're in there!" They hollered and pounded. "Come outside!" But Dad just kept praying.

And after a while, do you know what happened? The men went away again.

That was the second miracle.

Dad and Mom decided that we would be safer if we moved to a different house, so we packed everything into the car and left Abuja. We drove all day to Akure, where we moved into a new house with a really high fence around it. Akure is a lot smaller than Abuja, but the roads are still full of cars. Every time your car stops, people come to your window trying to sell you things to eat and drink. I liked it in Akure, but not because it reminded me of home. I liked it because Mom and Dad weren't working, so we all got to hang out together. But can you guess what happened?

That's right. One night Boko Haram found us.

Austin and I were asleep—we're really good sleepers, in case you hadn't figured it out yet. Again the men shouted and banged. They yelled that if Dad didn't come out, they would come in and take him.

Again, Dad prayed. But this time, he was even more nervous because the door they were banging on was not at all strong like the one we had in our home in Abuja. This one in Akure was made of thin wood and the locks were little. Dad figured that it would not take long before they broke it down and smashed their way inside. So he did the bravest thing I've ever known. He went outside. He ran out and slammed the back door behind him. Then he hid in the darkness behind a fence where he could see them banging on the front door. If they broke in the door, he was going to shout to them and give himself up so they would not come looking for Mom, Austin, or me.

But as he watched and prayed, something amazing happened. The men had heard all the noise that Dad made, and they thought it was the police coming to get them. So they ran away.

A third miracle.

I was asleep all those times when the men from Boko Haram visited us, but I was wide awake the day Dad told us that we were leaving Nigeria. It wasn't long after we had moved to the new house and Boko Haram had found us again. Dad and Mom were standing around when Austin and I were eating jollof rice for breakfast. For once it didn't taste so good, and my mouth didn't feel awake and alive. Mom and Dad looked so worried, and Austin asked them if they were okay. They said they were fine, but I wasn't so sure.

"Boys," said Dad as we started on the dishes. "We are going to take a very special vacation. We are going to America."

"America?" I whispered. I was so excited. I almost couldn't believe what he had just said. "Wow! What does it look like?"

"You'll see," Dad said. "We will stay with your cousins in Dallas. You won't even be able to count how many times you say *wow* because of all the sights in that country."

I had so many questions inside me: Where would we all sleep in Dallas? Were the cousins younger or older than me? What kinds of things did they like doing? It took a long time to ask them all.

It took two weeks before we could fly. I counted every day. Every night I went to sleep trying to imagine what it would be like to fly all the way to America and see so many of the things that I had seen in movies.

I had no idea what lay ahead—the good as well as the bad.

CHAPTER 3

FULL AND NOISY AND FUN

Mom was not born into an important family like Dad was. But her family was special and different and unlike any other family I know. Her dad had five wives and twenty children, and they all lived together in one house. Can you imagine that?

Mom says they all liked living with each other and that sharing her home with so many people taught her to be kind and loving. She's the most kind and loving person I know, so I guess she's right.

Mom and Dad are really different. Dad doesn't joke a lot, and he's always reminding us to make good choices in life. He's wise and brave, and I know that if I do what he says, life is going to be good. Mom is always smiling and laughing and joking and hugging us. If I ever feel sad or angry about the way someone has treated me, Mom's the person I go to for advice. I know that if I do what she says, any problems I have with someone can be fixed.

When we were living in Abuja, Mom worked at the bank each day while Austin and I were at school. I don't know what she did there, but she must have been really good at helping people. She was busy, but she always took us to school in the morning and walked us home at the end of the day. She'd cook and talk to us about homework and make sure that we'd done all our chores by the time Dad got home in the evening.

I loved it when we visited relatives, especially if they were Mom's sisters, brothers, or parents. The food was always super delicious, with amazing smells coming from the pans. I could close my eyes and feel my mouth start to water in seconds. The music was loud and fast, and there would be dancing until way into the night. And Mom would be right in the middle of them all, swaying and laughing and making sure everyone around her was having the best time.

Out of all of us, I think Mom was the saddest about leaving Nigeria.

I'd never heard of Dallas, and I'd never met Mom's uncle or his family, so I didn't have a clue what any of it would be like. It took us almost three days to make the journey, and I spent a lot of time asking Mom questions and thinking about it all. I imagined a big house full of people. I pictured us having parties that lasted into the night with good food and music and dancing. I ended up thinking that it was going to be a lot of fun. I was excited about it—maybe a little nervous too—but mainly really excited.

I got a few parts right.

The house was full of people and noise and food. As soon as we arrived, they fed us noodles and fish and rice. Mom and Dad laughed and smiled and looked really, really happy.

Mom's uncle and his wife—who we all called Grandma—were old, and they lived with some of their kids and grandkids. Austin and I shared a bedroom with two of the teenage boys, Damian and Terrell.

At first it was good. The first Sunday, we went to church, then ate spicy noodles and chicken and crispy duck in a Chinese restaurant. As we drove around in Grandma's big car, I couldn't stop staring at how big the stores and the trucks and the sidewalks all were.

The thing that amazed me the most was the lights. In Nigeria the lights are *always* going out. You can be watching TV or on your computer and then *bang*! Just like that, there's no more electricity in your house. Sometimes it can take weeks and weeks before the lights come back on again. But in America the lights hadn't gone out once.

But soon life became not so good in the house in Dallas. After we'd been there a few days, Terrell and Damian started complaining that Austin and I were moving their stuff.

I told Mom about it every time, and she always said the same thing. "Family can never be smooth all the time. All we can do is act in a loving way and try to get along."

I tried, but that's a really hard thing to do.

Mom's uncle said that we would be happier if we went to school. I wanted to tell him that I didn't really want to go to school, but I did not want to be disrespectful. Besides, at home in Nigeria, I always liked school. My teachers let me ask all my questions, and they would think really hard about the answers.

School in Dallas looked a lot different from school in Nigeria. The building was really big, and there were half as many children in the classes. Plus, we didn't have to squeeze all together on benches. Instead we had our own chairs and desks. And the lights in the ceiling were really bright and never went out once. I also liked the way the library was full of books and had so many computers that nobody had to share.

School was good, but not long after I started, two things happened and life in Dallas got bad. Not just kind of bad. Really bad.

The first thing was Dad. After I had been at school for two or three weeks, he told me that he was going back to Nigeria. I was sad and confused and worried. I didn't understand why he was going back already when we only just got here.

He said, "I need to go back so I can sell my machines and come back with enough money to live here."

I did not like it. I don't think Mom liked it either, because after he left, she started looking really worried and sad. Sometimes when I walked into her room, she tried to pretend that she had not just been crying.

The other problem was Damian and Terrell. Mom and Dad had told Austin and me to be really friendly to them. It worked for Austin, but it did not work for me. I tried to ask lots of questions, but they wouldn't talk to me. They'd stare at me like I was dirty. They'd kick my stuff around the bedroom. And then they started getting in my face about things.

There was one time when I was licking my finger because we had eaten candy and some of it was stuck on my fingernail.

Terrell walked up to me and hit me on the head. "Don't lick your finger around me, kid."

Mom saw. She was angry and shouted at him. "Why did you do that? We're family!"

Terrell looked at her as if he thought she was dirty just like me. "We're not family!"

Uncle came in then, and Terrell shouted and shouted and said things that I didn't believe a kid would *ever* say to an adult. But Terrell just kept shouting. I was waiting for Uncle to make Terrell stop, but he didn't. He just stood there, like he didn't mind being shouted at, and listened until Terrell was done.

The next time was worse.

Terrell was in the living room playing video games. I knew he did not want me to be watching him, so I was on the other side of the room playing with a Ping-Pong ball. I was rolling it along the floor and watching the way the draft from the doorway made it swerve.

I must have rolled the ball too hard because it went all the way over to Terrell and stopped when it touched his leg.

He looked at me. He put down his controller. He walked over to me. And then he got mad. He didn't just get a little mad. He got really mad. So mad that I got scared and started crying.

I ran and told Mom. She came and tried to put things right, but Terrell didn't listen. He didn't care that she was upset with him. He just kept on playing his video game.

That night Mom and I both cried, and I missed Dad more than ever.

CHAPTER 4

YOU WANNA PLAY CHESS?

Having an older brother like Austin is great. Well, most of the time it's great. When we lived in Abuja and played soccer in the courtyard with our friends, I often got upset with him. Let me explain.

Soccer is not an easy game when you're little and you're playing with your big brother and his big friends. And it's really hard when they don't pass you the ball, even though you stand on the side and wave your arms and shout over and over to them things like, "Hey! Pass me the ball!" or "I can *score* now! Pass it to me!"

Most of the time when this happened they'd ignore me. If I shouted as loud as I possibly could, they'd ignore me. And even when I started to cry, they'd still ignore me.

So that wasn't so good.

But when we moved to Akure and the house with the tall fence, playing soccer with Austin was more fun. None of our friends were around to play with us, so Austin *had* to pass the ball to me.

Soccer wasn't the only game we played at that house. One day Austin and I were both bored and he said, "Hey, I've got a great game we can play. Have you ever heard of chess?"

"No. What is it?"

"Go and ask Mom for some paper and scissors, and I'll show you."

So I got what we needed. I watched Austin cut up a whole bunch of squares of paper about as big as my pinkie nail. Then he got a bigger piece of paper and drew lots of lines on it. He told me to color every other square.

Austin showed me how to place my little pieces of paper on the squares. Then we took turns to move them one space forward at a time. It was sort of interesting, sort of not interesting. Mom came in and asked what we were doing.

"This is chess. I saw two of my teachers at school play it," Austin said.

Mom looked confused. "Shouldn't there be more than one kind of piece on the board?"

Austin said no, and we kept playing. I liked the way we took turns. And I liked that when it was my turn to go, I could stop and think and decide what to do. I didn't have to ask Austin to let me make my move. I could just make it.

Chess around the World

From Cuba to Russia, Iceland to India, and China to the United States, people all over the world love to play chess! In fact, 166 nations currently belong to the International Chess Federation. The federation hosts a world championship each year in a different country.

Some places are super into chess. Saint Petersburg, Russia, is filled with chess clubs and chess boards in public areas. The term *grand master* likely originates from a Russian tournament in 1914. Iceland is a tiny country with eight grand masters. The capital city, Reykjavik, hosted the famous world championship in which American Bobby Fischer triumphed over Russian Boris Spassky for the title in 1972. And chess is still a big deal in its birthplace, the Middle East: the United Arab Emirates has the largest chess club in the world.

People everywhere continue to love the challenge, strategy, and methodical play of chess. No matter where you are in the world, pull out your chess board. You're sure to find a worthy opponent, even if you don't speak the same language.

We played for a long time, until Austin said the game was over. I didn't know if I had won or not.

Everybody likes Austin. He's cool and knows stuff about science, like how many bones there are in the body and how long it takes for light to travel from the sun to the earth and why thunder and lightning happen. And he can play basketball with fully grown men and still do really well.

Our cousins in Dallas liked Austin more than they liked me. If he was in the living room when they were in there, they didn't mind so much. They even let him play video games with them. But if I even walked past them and touched them by accident, they'd start yelling that I wasn't allowed out of the bedroom and should go back there right now.

It wasn't just me they shouted at. They shouted at each other a lot. Sometimes they even shouted at Mom, even though she never did anything wrong.

I was confused about it all. It didn't make sense that young people talked to adults like this. It didn't make sense that family didn't act like family.

One night when I was going to bed, I told Mom that I didn't understand what was going on.

She smiled at me and said, "It's fine. Families are different, that's all. But we love each other, right?"

I thought for a moment. Mom always tells us "sorry goes a long way" and "let sorry be always in your mouth."

So I asked, "But do they say sorry to you for getting mad at you when you haven't even done anything?"

Mom shook her head. She waited awhile, like she was trying to find the right words. "But we can still forgive, can't we?" she asked.

I wanted to say "no!" and then go to sleep, but I knew she was right. Mom's always right about that kind of thing.

When she'd gone, it was just Austin and me in the room. Mom's words had helped, but I was still upset about it all. I could still feel the shouting inside me.

That's when Austin came and sat on my bed. He had a pair of scissors and some paper in his hands. "You wanna play chess?" he asked.

I don't think it's a miracle that I have Austin as my brother, but I do know this: he's the best brother ever.

CHAPTER 5

A NEW START

When Dad says, "Today is a new start for our family" on the bus to New York City, I know he is telling the truth. I know because I can always trust Dad. Ever since the men from Boko Haram started visiting us, Dad has told Austin and me that we don't need to worry and that everything will be okay. And even though we had to leave Nigeria, he's been right. Everything *has* been okay, and we haven't needed to worry.

And Dad *is* right because it doesn't take long before things start to change for us.

It starts as soon as we arrive in Queens, New York. We visit the house of one of Dad's friends from school. He's married and has lots of children and a really small house. At first I wonder if it's going to be the same as it was with Uncle and Grandma and Terrell and Damian. But Dad's friend is kind and funny. We spend the day eating and laughing and all playing together on the game console. Everyone gets a turn and nobody does any shouting.

We wake up laughing the next day too. This is because all four of us are sleeping in the same room, and in the morning, Dad starts snoring so loud that it sounds like there is a bus outside. It's hard to have a bad day when you wake up laughing so hard.

After breakfast we go to church. It's in Queens, near Dad's friend's house. And it isn't at all like church in Dallas. There I had to sit next to one of my cousins, and they would poke me and hit me if they got bored. It isn't like church back in Nigeria either. There are no metal detectors or guards at the doors in case Boko Haram attacks. It isn't even like a church at all. It's just a regular house on a regular street, and the church is down in the basement.

Dad wears a suit, and Mom puts on one of her bright dresses. In the tiny basement, people dressed just like Mom and Dad smile and say "hi!" Then one of the pastors starts calling out Bible verses, asking the kids to look them up as quick as they can. I even win a couple times. Nobody gives me any bad looks. They just keep smiling and treating us all well.

The main pastor is named Pastor Philip, and he is

extra nice. We're in his basement, and he makes everyone feel super welcome. He's so tall that he'd hit his head on the ceiling if he jumped. And even though everyone in the room is friendly, Pastor Philip has the biggest smile of all. He tells us that he is from the same part of Nigeria that we are from and that we are very welcome. I like him a lot.

The Great Big Yoruba Family

Tani's parents come from the Yoruba tribe, which is one of the largest ethnic groups in Africa. Approximately forty million people speak the Yoruba language.

People who belong to the Yoruba tribe value living as a close community. They are especially well-known for their respectful manners. Yoruba people take great pride in treating others well. If someone acts unkindly, the community will call out that person to protect the tribe's reputation for kindness.

Yoruba people are also extremely hospitable. They open their homes to visitors and people in need. They share food and possessions with their neighbors. It's common for extended families to live all together in the same house. To the Yoruba, family is the top priority—and everyone is treated like family!

After we finish church, we go upstairs to the kitchen. It's full of people cooking and laughing, and the air is steamy. It smells like it did whenever we spent the day with our cousins back home. We eat plates full of jollof rice and fried turkey, and it tastes just like it does when Mom cooks it. Did I tell you how great Nigerian food is?

But something else makes the day even better. While we are in church, it starts snowing!

I've seen snow before, but only on TV. Mom and Dad and Austin are the same. So when we've finished eating and have helped clean up, we all run outside.

The first weird thing I notice is that I don't feel as cold as I thought I would. Every time you see someone on TV in the snow, it always looks like they're freezing. But I actually get pretty hot when I am running around in the front yard of the church. Except for my hands—my hands go numb and stop feeling anything at all.

The other weird thing is how the snow feels. It's soft and hard at the same time. But I forget that snow is just frozen water, and soon my pants and hair and shoes are wet just like I've been out in the rain.

But the best thing is how much fun we have. Mom and Dad are with us outside, and they are laughing just as loud as Austin and I are. We're all patting the snow down and kicking it into the air, making it into balls and throwing it at each other. One of the kids from church shows Austin and me how to make snow angels, and we all lie down and make a whole row of angels right in front of the church. It's so, so great.

The only bad part is when my hands stop feeling numb and start feeling like they are on fire. I go back inside then, and it takes a long, long time for them to be warm again.

Church is over, but Pastor Philip says that we can stay in his house for as long as we need. He has a lot of other people staying in his house as well, so the only room we can sleep in is the basement where we had church. It's cold down there at night, and there isn't any carpet on the floor, just bare concrete. But Pastor Philip brings down so many blankets and pillows and cushions that we are able to get mostly warm.

Before we go to bed, we do what we always do at the end of every day: we pray. Mom and Dad start and then Austin and I join in. We sing some songs, then say sorry to God. Last we thank God for all the good things He has given us. Tonight there is *a lot* to thank Him for.

So the day ends just as it began. Mom and Dad and Austin and I are all in the same room, lying in our beds and laughing. We are talking about the snow and how much fun it was and how kind Pastor Philip was and how friendly everyone in church had been.

Then Austin asks a question that has just come into my mind as well. "Dad," he says. "What's going to happen tomorrow?"

Dad sits up, and I can see him clearly because there are no curtains on the window and there are streetlights shining outside. He's smiling and his eyes are wide, just like they were on the bus.

"Listen to me," he says, and Austin and I automatically sit up. "Tomorrow will be a great day. Tomorrow we begin our new life in New York City."

CHAPTER 6

THE HOTEL

It is cold and dark when we wake up the next morning. More snow has fallen in the night, and all our angels have been covered and hidden. But Pastor Philip is happy as he drives us in his car. He says he is taking us to a place full of people who can help us.

At first, I'm not so sure. It's a wide building that's all concrete and glass. When we get inside, we go to the back of a long line of people. But even though it's busy, everyone is quiet. Especially us.

We get called up, and Mom and Dad answer a lot of questions. I try to follow what they are saying, but it's hard to understand because the person they're listening to is talking really fast. Then we get sent away with some forms, and Mom and Dad have to work really hard to fill them in correctly.

"Sssssssh!" says Austin when I try and ask Mom a question. "They need to concentrate. It's like they're taking a really tough test."

So Austin and I sit quietly while Mom and Dad try and put the right answers in the boxes. Then there's a lot more waiting before we get called to visit another office. There are more questions to answer and more forms to fill out. Austin and I try really, really hard not to disturb anyone.

I spend a lot of the day looking out the window. It's busy on the street. The cars are always getting stuck and crawling along like they did back in Nigeria. But there are no people walking among them selling food or drink. All I can see on the street are cars and cars and more cars.

It's dark outside by the time we're told to visit another desk. I've lost count of the number of people we've seen or the number of forms Mom and Dad have filled out, so I sit down and wait on a bench with Austin. I feel myself falling asleep.

I wake up when I hear Dad and Mom talking loudly. "Tonight? Are you sure?"

I can't hear what the person behind the desk is saying, but I can see the side of Mom's face. Her eyes are shining, and she looks like she might be about to cry—but not because she's sad. She looks happy, happier than I have seen her in a long time. "Thank you!" she says over and over.

Dad comes over and explains to us what is going on. "Pastor Philip was right. These are good, good people. And they have agreed to help us."

"How?" Austin and I say at the same time.

"They are giving us a home."

I look at Austin. He looks as confused and surprised as I feel. I want to ask Dad some more questions, but his phone rings. It's Pastor Philip.

Dad tells him the news. "We have been told that we are going to be housed in a shelter. Is that like a tent?"

I don't hear what Pastor Philip is saying, but a smile spreads across Dad's cheeks. "That's good," he says. He's looking at a piece of paper that the person at the desk gave him. "Where is Manhattan? We really want to be near you and the church."

Dad listens some more. "Thirtieth Street, Park Avenue," he says.

This time I can hear exactly what Pastor Philip says. He's shouting, "Whoa! God is blessing you mightily. Park Avenue is the best street in the whole city. And you're going to be living there. Praise God!"

We have to wait some more before someone can drive us to our new home. I'm excited at first, but by the time we carry our bags out into the night and load them onto the bus, the elephant is back in my stomach.

Our bus takes us into the heart of New York City. I've never seen buildings so tall or so many lights. It's dark and late and cold, but the streets are still full of cars, and there are people on the sidewalks. I press my forehead against the freezing window glass and look up, but some of the buildings are so tall that I can't even see their tops.

The bus slows, and we stop on the side of a street that's wider than any I've ever seen. Before we stand, Dad says he has something to tell us.

"When I was younger, my father always told me this one thing: *know where you come from.* Whatever lies ahead, let us not forget who we are or where we come from. Let us choose always to be polite and respectful, to be kind and generous. Let us not forget that we are the grandson and great-grandsons of a king. Let us show our appreciation for this blessing by being a blessing to others. Do you agree?"

"A-men," I say at the same time as Mom and Austin. "Amen! Amen!"

We walk inside the building with big smiles and wide eyes. Dad calls this place a shelter, but the sign outside says it's a hotel. I can't believe it. We're actually living in a hotel! There are glass doors and big fabric chairs and even an elevator that takes us all the way up to the seventh floor.

We walk down the hall to an office where a woman

named Jacki tells us the rules. "First, curfew is 9:00 p.m. If you aren't signed in by nine for three nights running, then you're out. Second, no alcohol. If we find that you've brought any alcohol into your room or anywhere in the facility, you're gone."

I don't know what *curfew* means, but Mom and Dad are nodding, so I guess it's not a bad thing.

Jacki keeps on talking. "It's the same with smoking, drugs, or using anything hot like an iron or a stove in your room. You can't do that. It's forbidden and you've got to make sure your boys understand that too. If we catch you, you're gone."

Austin and I are nodding too. I don't know if Jacki ever smiles, but it's hard to imagine what she would look like if she did. She's serious and has this way of frowning that makes me want to stand up straight. Jacki is the kind of person I absolutely do not want to get in trouble with. I think that if she got mad and started shouting, it would be terrifying.

"We serve three meals a day, but those times are strict. If you miss the mealtime, you miss the meal."

I'm so glad we get to eat in the Hotel that I stop listening to what Jacki's saying for a moment. It's something about how we have to sign in and out and ask them to unlock our room every time we come back. I don't mind. I'm just excited that we're here.

When Jacki has finished explaining all the rules, she

takes us to our rooms. Austin and I are together in a room on the fifth floor, and Mom and Dad are in a room on the fourth floor.

My room is small. The walls and the covers on the bed are all the same color brown. It's only just large enough for two narrow beds with a small gap between them. There are some drawers and a small bathroom and a window that looks out onto the street below. I guess it will be cool to have a bathroom for just me and Austin. But it all feels so different from any place I've lived before.

This is a room, not a home.

I stare at the lights while Mom tries to get me ready for bed. She says I don't have to bathe, but I do have to brush my teeth and wash my face. She's almost done turning the covers down when I have a question that I need to ask.

"Mom, how can we afford to live here? Isn't it expensive to stay in a hotel?"

She smiles. "Hotels are expensive; you're right. But this is not costing us anything."

"Why not?"

"Because the people of America are kind," Mom says. "They are paying for us to stay here."

I look at Austin. He's just as amazed as me.

"Really?" he says.

Mom nods. "Really. The people we were with today are part of the government. If a family doesn't have a home, they will provide one."

"Wow!" I say. "That's really generous."

We all pray then. There's a lot to thank God for—again!

When we have said "amen," Mom goes. For a moment I feel worried because I can't remember where her and Dad's room is. At home I could just walk down the hall and find them. And in Dallas they slept next door. I've never slept so far away from them.

Austin comes and sits on my bed. "Hey," he says. "It's okay. Remember what Dad said about this being a new start?" I nod. "We don't have to be scared. We can trust him and Mom. And we can trust God too. Have any of them let us down yet?"

I shake my head.

Austin continues. "We're safe, we've got a new home, and there are people who are going to look after us. I'd call that another miracle, wouldn't you?"

Austin is right. I feel better.

I look out the window at the city, which is filled up with lights. I remember the way the lights were always going out at home. But here it's different. I've never seen so many lights. They're so bright, and there are so many of them that even if I stayed awake all night, I could never count them all. Here in New York, everything seems to work.

CHAPTER 7

THE BEST THING EVER

I half wake up, and for a moment before I open my eyes, I forget where we are. Are we in Queens in the church? Or are we in the house of Dad's friend? I can hear traffic outside. Is it Dallas? Akure? Abuja?

Then I remember the Hotel and the wide road outside filled with traffic. I remember that it's the second morning we're living in the Hotel, that we're safe, and that there are good people around who have promised to help us. It feels good to remember all this.

And then I feel bad because I remember something else. This morning Mom is taking me to start at my new school.

I like school. I've always liked school. But when you've only just arrived in a new place and you don't have any friends, it's hard to get excited about going to school.

I felt this way in Dallas when Mom told me that Austin and I were going to start school there. We'd only been in Grandma's house four or five days, and I didn't feel ready.

And now we've only been in New York City for two days. I feel even worse.

I have to wait for Austin to wake up. (Believe me, you *don't* want to wake up my brother early in the morning. Not unless you want to be shouted at by a sleep-eyed, angry monster.) So once I'm dressed and my teeth are clean, I look out the window at the cars crawling by below. Then Austin's alarm goes off, he dresses super fast, and we ride the elevator down to Mom and Dad's room on the floor below.

Dad's wearing a suit. "Why are you dressed like that, Dad?" I ask. He likes suits and he looks really handsome in them, but I have not seen him wear one since we were living in Abuja and he was working at his printing shop.

"You're not the only ones who are starting your new life here in New York City," he says. "Pastor Philip has arranged for me to have a job interview. It is important to make a good impression."

We all go back up to the seventh floor to eat breakfast.

I don't recognize much of the food they have on the tables, but Mom helps me choose a muffin and a juice box. But I'm not hungry. My elephant is back.

My school is called PS 116, and it is on East Thirty-Third Street. It takes ten minutes to walk there from the Hotel. As we walk, Mom tells us the things we need to know.

"I know that it is not always easy to go into a new school, but do you remember what Dad said the night we arrived in the city?"

"Yes," I say. "Know where you come from."

"That's right. You both will do well if you remember that. If anyone offends you, don't talk back. Report it to your teacher or the supervisor at recess or me if you need to. Just don't disrespect anybody, no matter if they are younger or older. And always be the first to apologize. *Sorry* goes a long way. And if someone says 'sorry' to you and you're still complaining, what else do you want? It's a powerful word; let it be in your mouth."

Mom had said the same words when we started school in Dallas. I guess she probably said the same words when we started school in Nigeria. I don't mind. I like it. Mom and Dad always give good advice. I can trust them.

Before we reach my new school, we take Austin to his. I stand outside and stare. It doesn't look like a school.

In Dallas I could recognize the schools immediately. They looked a lot like they did in Nigeria, with trees and sports fields and lots of space to run around in. But Austin's school in New York City is a tall building with a fence that's so high and no trees anywhere.

We say goodbye to Austin and walk to PS 116. Mom keeps on talking, but I'm not listening. I'm thinking that if Austin's school looks different outside, then it must be different inside as well. I hope that my school doesn't look that way.

There's no fence at my new school, but the windows are so high that I can't see in them from the street. There's a big red door with a hand-painted sign that says PS 116. My stomach flips, and I wish I was back in bed.

Mom takes my hand and squeezes it. She's giving me a smile that makes me feel better and braver and just a *little* bit less nervous.

"Okay," she says. "Ready?"

I swallow hard and nod. "Ready."

It doesn't take long for me to feel better. The teachers are kind and smile at me when they talk. When there's recess, I am taken outside with the other kids, and everyone I talk to is friendly. They ask me questions about Nigeria and Dallas, and I tell them what I can remember.

I also ask them a lot of questions.

Profile: Nigeria

Population: 203,452,505 (2018 est.)

Government: federal republic; citizens elect politicians every four years, including the president

Capital City: Abuja (2,440,200 population in 2019); nicknamed "Africa's Big Apple"

Religion: Most Nigerians are either Christian or Muslim.

Languages: English (official), Hausa, Igbo, Yoruba, and over 500 other tribal languages

Size: 356,669 square miles

Sports: Nigerians go crazy for soccer. Basketball and boxing are also popular.

Industry: Nigeria has the largest economy in Africa. It exports oil, gas, beans, cashews, and sesame. It also has a thriving film industry, called Nollywood. Each week as many as two hundred movies are produced in Nigeria!

Fast Facts

The highest point in Nigeria is Chappal Waddi, a mountain that is 7,936 feet tall.

Nigeria has more kinds of butterflies than anywhere else in the world.

"What else do you do at recess?"

"Do you like all the teachers the same, or are some nicer than others?"

"Where are the bathrooms?"

I listen carefully to all of their answers and try to remember every word. It's hard because some of the recess games they talk about I've never heard of, and I don't know the names of the teachers yet. But there is one answer I do not have to struggle to remember. When I ask one kid what his favorite subject is, he doesn't hesitate.

"Chess," he says, smiling big. "It's the best thing ever."

CHAPTER 8

MOVING
FORWARD

One morning, not long after I've started school, I am waiting on the seventh floor for Mom and Austin to come and sign out when a lady named Miss Maria looks out from the office down the hall.

"Hey, Tani," she says. "Come here."

I wonder if I've broken one of the rules and am in trouble, but Miss Maria is smiling. Besides, Dad and Mom like Miss Maria a lot. They are always asking her questions and getting her advice on what to do about things.

I get to her office and wait in the doorway. She's still smiling and holding out a box with one donut in it. "You want it?" she says. "It's got jelly inside. I bought it for you."

I give her my biggest smile possible, say "thank you," and reach out for the donut. It tastes *sooooo* good.

A Nigerian Feast

As Tani says, Nigerian food is the best food in the world. If you are invited to a Nigerian feast, you might find some of these delicious dishes.

Pounded yam: White African yams beaten into a
doughy mash and rolled into balls
Jollof rice: White rice simmered with tomatoes,
peppers, onions, curry, and thyme
Turkey stew: A thick soup of smoked turkey,
peppers, tomatoes, and onions, seasoned with
curry and ginger
Akara: Crispy fried cakes made from black-eyed peas,
onions, and spices
Suya: Kebabs of spiced beef and onions
Dodo: Plantains fried to a golden brown and seasoned
with onions and lime
Zobo: Sweet and tangy tea made from roselle flowers,
served iced
Puff puff: Sweet dough balls fried and tossed in sugar

I think Mom and Dad need donuts too. They're both so tired from working hard. Dad has a job washing dishes and pans in a restaurant. He leaves after we have eaten our evening meal in the Hotel, rides the subway for an hour, and spends *all night* cleaning. He arrives back in the morning just when we're eating breakfast. As soon as he has eaten, he goes back to his room and sleeps while Austin and I go to school. I have never seen him looking this tired.

Mom is working hard too. Austin and I don't like the food they serve at the Hotel. It doesn't have a lot of flavor, there's no spice like we're used to, and there's *a lot* of cheese. I don't like cheese that much. I do like the cookies and the muffins, especially the ones with chocolate. But cheese? I just don't get it.

Mom decided that it's not good for Austin and me to eat only cookies and muffins, so she has started to cook our own meals. The only problem is that we're not allowed to cook in the Hotel, so Mom has to go to someone else's home to use their kitchen. And the nearest person we know with a kitchen is Pastor Philip, outside the city in Queens.

It takes Mom two hours to get to Pastor Philip's house. She has to ride two trains and one bus, and she has to work fast as she cooks and then cleans the kitchen. Then she brings all the meals she has made back with her to the Hotel.

By the time she returns, we're all gathered in her and Dad's room, sitting on his bed. She opens the containers in her shopping carts and tells us what she has made. "Jollof rice . . . pounded yam . . . turkey stew . . ." All the things she made in Nigeria. All the things we love. As she chooses a container and opens it up, the room fills with my favorite smells. My mouth starts to water, and I have to sit on my hands to try and keep still.

Eventually we all have plates of delicious food on our laps. We pray to say thanks to God, then eat. None of us talk. It's too tasty for words!

Dad works six nights each week. Sometimes he even works seven nights. And Mom cooks in Pastor Philip's kitchen three times each week. When we sit on Dad's bed and eat, they both look tired. But I know they are happy too. Mom says, "I love cooking, and I love watching you all eat so happily. Feeling tired is worth it."

Dad says, "I am tired, but how can I not be happy? We are alive and well. We are safe from harm. And tonight I will have another opportunity to go out to work and keep my family moving forward."

So I'm grateful for my parents. They're kind and they work hard. And thanks to the money Dad earns and the time Mom spends cooking, my belly is full of good food that makes me feel like home is not so far away after all.

But they're busy. And that means that Austin and I have a lot of time to ourselves. And because there's nowhere else to go, we spend a lot of time in our room. And sometimes I feel bored.

That's okay though. I can deal with feeling bored.

What I don't like are the times when I feel scared.

CHAPTER 9

STRONG STARES AND CROCODILE TEETH

Not everyone in the Hotel is nice like Miss Maria.

Sometimes if Mom is cooking at Pastor Philip's house and Dad has to go to work early, Austin gets me from school and we go back to the Hotel together.

One day Austin and I have just gotten back and we're waiting for the elevator to come down, then take us up to the seventh floor, when a man walks up to us.

He looks like his face is made of leather and his hair is made of string. He's not much taller than Austin, and he's really skinny, like he hasn't eaten a meal in over a year. He's staring at us both, smiling. It's not the kind of smile that warms up my insides. It reminds me of a crocodile's jagged mouth.

"What are you two doing on your own?"

Austin says nothing. I open my mouth to talk, but Austin stares at me and I can't think of anything to say.

The elevator arrives and Austin and I get in. The man joins us.

"So," he says once Austin presses the button marked 7 and we start moving upward. "Where are your parents, boys? Are they home?"

The man is staring right at me, and I can't look away. He's like a magician or something. I wish the elevator wasn't quite so small. I'm praying that the ride will be over soon.

His eyes are strong, staring right at me. I shake my head. This makes his smile go wide, and his voice gets loud.

"Your parents aren't *home*? That's *wrong*! You should call your parents *right now* and have them come back here to take care of you."

Austin reaches out for my hand and holds it tight. And when the elevator stops and we get out and walk toward the office together, the man stays in the elevator and goes to a different floor.

"You just need to stay quiet," says Austin as we walk. "Don't look people like that in the face. Wait until they've finished; they always get bored soon enough as long as you don't give them a reaction."

We see the man again a few days later, when Austin and I are leaving the dining room together. My heart is racing. The man says the same things, but this time I do what Austin says and stare at the floor. It doesn't take long for the man to give up and leave us.

We don't see the man after that, and I never knew what happened to him.

As the weeks go by, other people who are like him move into the Hotel and want to get into our business. Some ask us why we're alone. Others ask us where we're from. But I try not to listen to what they're saying too much. Some are men, some are women, but none of them seem to last very long in the Hotel. They get thrown out because they're caught with beer in their rooms or they miss the curfew three nights in a row. Part of me is relieved when they go. But I also feel sad for them. Do they have another hotel to go to? I hope so.

The most important thing I learn in all of this is about my brother. Austin is one of the kindest people on the planet. He is patient and good at teaching me things. And he's wise too. Everyone should have a big brother like him.

Although, he could be a little less grouchy in the mornings when he wakes up.

CHAPTER 10

SO THAT'S HOW YOU PLAY CHESS!

In New York, they like chess so much that they have chess lessons in regular school. So one day, just before recess, I have my first chess lesson. I think I know how to play chess because I can remember most of what Austin taught me when we made our own set out of paper in Akure. But even before the lesson starts, I can tell that Austin's chess is different from the chess we're going to play at PS 116. Nobody's cutting up any pieces of paper with scissors. Instead there are all these little statues lined up on wooden boards: black statues on one side, white on the other.

I want to pick up one of the statues. But I don't because there's a man standing at the front of the room who I've not seen before.

Everyone who comes in smiles at him and says, "Hi, Coach Shawn." He smiles and says hi back. Then he tells us all to sit down because it's time to start.

I don't know what a typical chess coach should look like, but Coach Shawn doesn't look like any of my other teachers. He's wearing the kind of sneakers that Austin points out when we walk past shoe stores, the sort that you wear for basketball. And Coach Shawn talks different too. He doesn't talk loud or sound like he's trying to test us or trick us or work out what we don't know. When he talks, it sounds like he's talking about his favorite thing. He must love chess more than anything in the world.

But I don't understand everything he says. He's using words that I've not heard before, like "pawns . . . openings . . . checkmate." I want to hold my hand up and ask, but I feel too shy. So I sit and stare at Coach Shawn and listen as hard as I can.

"When you're playing chess, you're fighting a battle," says Coach Shawn. "Lots of battles in fact."

I like what he says. And when I pick up the biggest piece on the board in front of me, I like the way it feels. It's strong. Unbreakable.

When he's done talking, Coach Shawn tells everyone to start playing. I don't know what to do, but he comes over to me and says hi. Then he asks, "Have you played before?"

"I don't know," I say. I'm not going to tell him about Austin's version of chess.

"That's okay. I'm going to put you with Jack. He hasn't been playing long either. He'll show you what to do."

Jack goes first and moves a piece. I pick up the tallest piece and start to move it, but Jack shakes his head. "You can't do that!"

I try moving one of the pieces on the edge of the board, but he says, "Illegal!" So I just move the same piece that he did. I do this for the next few moves, just copying whatever Jack does. It's not much of a battle.

"Checkmate!" says Jack.

I look at him. "What's that?"

"It's over. I won."

Right now, I don't like chess. It's confusing, and I don't like it at all.

But Coach Shawn comes over and squats down on the floor next to my chair. He's smiling at me, and I can't help smiling back.

"It looks complicated at first, doesn't it?"

I nod. "I don't know how to play," I say. But as I'm looking at all the pieces and listening to all the people and seeing Coach Shawn squatting next to me, I think that it would be cool to be able to play.

"Don't worry, Tani. Everyone else here has been playing for at least three months. They know more than you do right now. But we can change that. I'm going to show you how each piece moves. If you pay attention and remember what they do, you might be able to play in about two weeks."

"I'd like that," I say.

So I pay attention. I pay really, really good attention. First, Coach Shawn explains that the goal of chess is to capture the other player's king. He shows me the king; it's the tallest piece and has a cross on top. Then Coach Shawn picks up each of the other pieces, tells me its name, and shows me the way it is allowed to move. He says that the queen is the most powerful piece because she can move any direction and any number of spaces. I make my brain remember everything. I lock it inside of me, deep down.

Coach Shawn puts down the last piece and looks at me. "You got all that?"

I nod hard.

"You want me to go over anything?"

"No."

"Well okay then." He smiles. "I'll see you next lesson, Tani. Try and remember as much as you can."

I nod and smile, but I don't look at him. I'm too busy staring at the board, reminding myself of all the pieces and how they move.

CHAPTER 11

"YES, COACH SHAWN!"

I try hard to remember everything that Coach Shawn told me about the way the different pieces move. When I'm going to sleep or when I'm waiting for the elevator or when I'm sitting on my bed in the afternoon, chess is all I think about. I picture Coach Shawn sitting beside me, picking up each piece in turn, and telling me everything I need to know about it.

Pawns are easy to remember. So are the king and the queen. The way knights move by jumping over other pieces is strange, so I never have any problem remembering those. But I get confused between bishops and rooks. One of them moves on a diagonal, the other moves along straight lines. Which one does which?

So I'm feeling my elephant at the start of my second

lesson with Coach Shawn. I'm worried that he will want to give me a test to see how well I was listening to him in our first lesson. What if I make a mistake? What if I fail?

Right before the start of the lesson, when everyone is getting their boards set up, he comes over. "Hey, Tani. You okay?"

"Yes, Coach Shawn." I'm really worried now because other people are watching.

"Can you remember any of the pieces and how they move?"

"Um . . ." I say. "I guess. Do you want me to show you?"

"Sure!"

I pick up my favorite piece. "This is the king. He can move in any direction, but only one square at a time."

Coach Shawn smiles and nods, so I pick up another one. "This is the queen and she can move any number of spaces she wants in any direction. These knights move funny, always in an L shape, two spaces in one direction then one to the side. They can jump, too, which is cool. Pawns only get to move forward one space, but they can move two spaces on the first move. Pawns are the only pieces that capture differently from how they move. They can only capture an enemy piece if it's diagonally in front of them."

I stop talking. I can't remember which one's the rook and which one's the bishop. But Coach Shawn is smiling.

"Tani, that's good. Really good. Did anyone help you remember them?"

I shake my head.

He continues looking at me, and his smile gets bigger. Then he holds out his hand, gives me a fist bump, and calls everyone to pay attention for the lesson.

"All right, all right, all right," he says. "Listen up. I've got a riddle for you. You ready?"

Everyone shouts out, "Yes, Coach Shawn!"

"Okay, so can you guys name something that has four legs in the morning, two in the afternoon, and three at night?"

Almost everyone holds a hand up. Coach Shawn picks on people to speak. Some of the answers are pretty funny.

"An elephant!"

"A bed!"

"A rocket that got busted!"

Coach Shawn is laughing like the rest of us. The answers keep coming, and soon I'm laughing so hard I can't even hear them.

"Okay, okay," says Coach Shawn. "I'll tell you. It's a human being."

Some people are confused and say, "What?"

"When you're a baby you crawl, so you've got four legs. Then when you're older, it's like the afternoon of your life and you walk with two feet. When you get real old, you're going to need a cane, so that's why humans have three legs in the evening of life."

I get it. It's really clever.

Next Coach Shawn talks about chess, so I listen extra hard. I even move places so that I can be right in the front row to see him up close. I want to hear every word.

"We've been working for three months now, and you all know the moves of the pieces, but I've got to tell you that knowing the moves is not enough. The concept of the game is a lot deeper. If you want to be good at chess, you've got to learn how to make good decisions."

Then he says something strange. "Raise your hand if you know how to cross the street."

I put mine up in the air, but I check to make sure it's not a trick. Everyone else has a hand up too.

Coach Shawn nods. "Right. Is it simple or difficult to cross the street?"

"It's simple!" The class answers all together.

"Okay, but if one day you forget what to do when you're crossing the street, and you forget to look both ways and make that mistake, what could happen to you?"

I have my hand up high. Mom talks to me a lot about crossing the street ever since we moved to the Hotel because the roads in New York are a *lot* busier than they are in Dallas or most places in Nigeria. When Coach Shawn calls on me, I say, "You'd be hit by a car and you might die."

"That's right, Tani. Even a simple thing like crossing the street can have really bad consequences for your life. And that's like chess. You might think you're just making a simple move, so you can make it fast and not think about it carefully. But you can end up in so much trouble. You've got to think the consequences through. You've got to think deep. Otherwise you're going to end up in trouble."

I like everything that Coach Shawn says. Everything. He's like a teacher, only better. He's clever *and* fun at the same time.

And that's when I know that I really, really want to be a chess player.

At the end of the lesson, Coach Shawn calls me over. "We run an after-school chess program, Tani. I think you'd like it." He gives me a letter to take back to Mom and Dad, and I say, "Thank you."

I'm so excited about chess that as soon as I see Mom, I give her the letter. She looks at it, frowns, and quickly puts it away in her bag. I want to ask her about going to the after-school program, but I can tell that this is not a good time to ask. So instead I decide to tell her all about Coach Shawn.

"Coach Shawn says that some people like chess because it's competitive. They like winning. And if you do like forty or fifty chess puzzles each week and go to practice and work hard, you will get better. But some people like it because maybe they're not good at sports or have never been on a team, so when they join the chess program, they're part of a real team that goes to tournaments and competes together. Some people like chess because they like the way they have to do what Coach Shawn calls deep thinking."

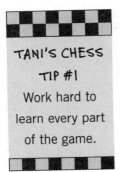

TANI'S CHESS TIP #1
Work hard to learn every part of the game.

"Wait, Tani!" she says, grabbing my backpack as I step into the street. The sound of the car horn is so loud in my ear that it almost hurts. "The light's not green yet."

"Sorry, Mom." I step back beside her as I continue. "Coach Shawn says that deep thinking is when you have to make your brain concentrate harder than you've ever made it concentrate before and imagine all the possible moves that could follow when you make a certain move. Coach Shawn says that with practice, you can do deep thinking so good that you can see four or five moves ahead."

"Okay. So which of those reasons is the main one behind you wanting to play?"

That's a good question. It takes me a long time to find the answer. "All of them."

"All of them?" she says.

"Yes. Coach Shawn says that chess is not a game you just pick up. He says you've got to understand it all, every part of it, and to do that you have to make sacrifices. But if you do that and work hard, then you can go far."

When the light shows that we can cross the street, we walk a little farther without talking. Then I can't wait any longer.

"Mom," I say. "Can I go to the after-school chess program?"

She looks at me and smiles, but it's not one of her big smiles that I see when she's in a room full of people. It's still a smile, but it looks sad.

"Tani, it's a lot of money. More than Dad earns in a week. But . . ."

"It's okay, Mom," I say, even though I don't feel okay.

"Let me see what I can do, okay?"

I nod and smile back at her. My smile probably looks a little sad, just like hers.

CHAPTER 12

I'M A CHESS PLAYER

This is the best day ever.

It starts when Mom picks me up from school. She has a smile on her face that is all happiness and no worry at all. "I have a present for you," she says.

"What? What is it?"

"You'll have to wait until we get back. It's waiting for you in your bedroom."

"What?" I say, laughing. "Tell me, Mom. What is it?"
She refuses.

All the way back to the Hotel I try to get her to tell me, but she won't. I try guessing too, but the only thing she says is, "Just wait."

By the time we get to my room, I am so excited that I am almost shaking. And as soon as we get inside and I see the present sitting on my bed, I turn around and give Mom the biggest hug I've ever given her *in my life*!

It's probably the best present I've ever received. It's even better than the pilot pin I got when we flew to America.

It's a chess set.

I open the paper box, unfold the board, and take out the cool plastic pieces, one by one. I have a chess set of my own!

"Is it right?" says Mom. "I'm sorry we could not afford a better one."

"It's perfect," I say, grinning.

The day gets even better when Austin comes back. I show him the board and his eyes go wide as he says, "That's cool."

"Do you want to play?" I ask.

Other brothers might say no. They might not want their kid brother teaching them a game that they tried to teach before. But Austin isn't like other brothers. Even when we have a big fight because he's pulled my covers off in the morning to get me out of bed and I have suddenly gotten so cold that my feet turn to *ice*, we always make up within a maximum of two hours. We both like it when everything is good between us.

"Sure," says Austin as he sits down on the bed with the board between us.

I tell him everything I know about all the pieces and how they move. Austin listens hard, and then we play.

I win, but I don't think he feels bad about that. He just stares at the pieces on the board, and I can tell that he's doing exactly what Coach Shawn tells us to do.

"You're deep thinking," I say.

He looks up at me, confused. "What?"

"You're looking at the board, and you're trying to see the different moves. Coach Shawn says that's really important."

Austin shrugs. Then he sets up the board. "Let's play again."

We play another game and then another. We only stop when Mom comes to our room to tell us to come and eat.

"I have some news for you," Mom says when we sit down on Dad's bed and she starts spooning the pounded yam and stew on the plates. "I have been emailing Coach Russ."

For a moment I'm confused. "Coach Russ?" I don't know who that is.

"The one who runs the after-school chess program with Coach Shawn."

My heart beats faster. Even though I'm holding a plate of some of my favorite food, I don't eat. I just stare at Mom, waiting for her to explain more.

How to Play Chess

The object of the game is to capture your opponent's king.

Setup

1. Position the board between the players. A light-colored square should be at the bottom-right corner in front of each player.
2. Place the pieces on the board. On the row closest to each player, place (from left to right) a rook, a knight, a bishop, the queen, the king, a bishop, a knight, and a rook. Line up the pawns on the second row.
3. White moves first. Then the players take alternating turns.

How to Move Each Piece

The **king** is the most valuable piece. The king moves one square in any direction.

The **queen** is the most powerful piece. The queen can move any number of squares in any direction.

Knights move three squares at a time, in an L-shaped pattern. Knights can jump over other pieces.

Bishops move diagonally. They can move any number of squares at a time.

Rooks, or castles, move any number of squares forward, back, or across (but not diagonally).

Pawns usually move only one square forward. However, they can capture an opposing piece by moving one square forward *diagonally*. For its first move, each pawn can move two squares forward. Pawns can never move backward.

Other Rules

Capturing: A piece is captured when it is in the direct path of the opponent's moving piece. The only exception is pawns, which capture with diagonal moves.

Promoting a pawn: When a pawn reaches the opposite end of the board, it can become any piece. This is called *promotion*.

How to End the Game

Checkmate: A player wins when their opponent's king cannot move out of danger of being captured.

Draw: When the players agree that neither can win, a draw is called. A draw can happen if the only available move is to move the king into danger. A draw can also happen if both players decide they are done trying, if the same position is repeated three times, or if fifty consecutive moves have been made without either player moving a pawn or capturing a piece.

"I asked Coach Russ if you could join the program. Do you still want to?"

"Yes," I say. "But it is expensive."

"I explained that we could not pay even though we want to. But Coach Russ says you can join the club anyway. No need to pay."

I am surprised and excited all at the same time. I almost drop my plate as I jump up to give Mom a hug.

Later that night, long after we have said good night to Mom, Austin and I play another game of chess. The board is on the floor between the two beds, and we're both squeezed in tight.

I'm tired but I don't want to go to sleep. I want to keep playing. I wish I could stay up all night like this and never have to sleep.

"Checkmate."

"What?" I say.

Austin is staring at the board, smiling. "It's checkmate. You can't move your king without putting him in check."

I stare at the pieces. I look at my king and work through all the possible moves I could make. Then I look at the other pieces and do the same. But Austin's right. The game's over. He's won.

I hold out my hand the way I've seen other players do and shake Austin's. "Well done," I say. "You played well."

And I have the strangest feeling inside, like I'm happy

and sad at the same time. I don't like that I've lost, but I like that Austin has won.

"Again?" I say.

Austin yawns and says he wants to go to sleep. "But we'll play tomorrow, okay?"

I go to bed too, but I don't go to sleep.

Even with the blinds down, it's bright in the room from all the streetlights outside. The city is not at all tired. It's awake and alive and my brain feels the same.

I've got a chessboard, I've got someone to play with, and I've got a place in a chess club. I'm a chess player.

I don't know if that counts as a miracle, but it sure feels like one.

CHAPTER 13

YOU CAN TOO

It's Thursday, 2:30 p.m. School has just finished, but I am not leaving. I'm sitting in the classroom. My first chess program is about to start!

Some of the other kids are wearing blue T-shirts that have *PS 116 NYC* on them. The letters are drawn in a way that makes chess pieces across the top. It's cool. One day I'd like to have one.

I can see Coach Shawn, but he's talking with a man I've not seen before. He's taller than Coach Shawn, but he has the same smile where his eyes get narrow and sparkly.

The room is full of kids from school, and it's loud. I feel small and nervous too. What if they ask me to play and I lose? Can I still belong to the chess program if I'm not good?

"Okay," says the man I've not seen before, checking his watch. "We're going to start now. Hi, everyone."

A bunch of people call out, "Hey, Coach Russ," and Coach Russ begins.

For the first few seconds all I can think is that Coach Russ and Coach Shawn are very different. Coach Shawn is soft-spoken and looks like he's always concentrating on everything he says. He talks like every word is a great chess move. Coach Russ is the opposite. He talks fast and his eyes are full of light and life. He's standing at the front of the classroom, and everyone is listening. I can feel that they are all excited and full of energy.

"I want to tell you something," Coach Russ says. "Make it your goal to always fight to improve every day. Come to every practice eager and willing, be ready to participate and hungry to become a better player every time you sit down at a board or open up a chess puzzle. The people who do the best in chess are the ones who work the hardest. It's not about where you live or what kind of resources you've got. Anyone can be good. All you need is the will and the passion."

I think I understand what he's saying, but I'm not sure. So I listen even harder as he continues.

"One of the best players I ever worked with grew up in the South Bronx, right here in New York City. His family didn't have much money, so he didn't have access to lots of coaches. But he watched a lot of chess videos on

YouTube. He worked hard, he practiced, and he studied how to become a better player. And do you know what happened? Within less than three years, he went from never playing to becoming one of the youngest American chess masters. Right now he's studying at one of the best universities in the world. And if he can get so good by being determined and working hard, then don't you think you can too?"

Some people say yes and others start moving in their seats. But not me. I don't say anything, and I don't move a single muscle. I'm listening to the yes that I'm shouting inside of me.

I don't just want to be a chess player. I want to be the *best* chess player I can possibly be.

CHAPTER 14

SNEAKERS AND ROSA PARKS

Every day that we go to school, Miss Maria has a donut that she gives either to Austin or to me. I don't think she hands out donuts to other people because I've never seen her do it. But maybe she does. Maybe she gives them when nobody else is looking. Maybe she likes to be kind and generous without lots of people finding out about it.

One day I'm waiting for Mom and Austin, when I hear Miss Maria calling out. "Is that an Adewumi boy out there in the corridor? Because right about now's the time when one of those boys usually comes knocking on my door *demanding* that I give him something, and the *only* way I can get rid of him is by giving him a donut."

Miss Maria is always joking like this. She pretends that she's frustrated or mad or whatever with Austin and me, but whenever she looks at us, she always has this superwide smile on her face. I like her a lot, and it's not just because of the donuts or the fact that she makes me smile. I like her because she has the same smile on her face when she's talking with Mom and Dad too. They're always asking her questions about Dad's job or things in the shelter or how long we can stay in America, and Miss Maria listens and explains things to them and helps them understand what's going on.

Mom and Dad are always talking about the advice she's given them, saying how helpful she is and how much they appreciate her. It reminds me of the way I feel about Coach Shawn. It's good to have someone wise who can help you in life.

On the day that I'm standing outside the elevator and Miss Maria calls out and teases me about *demanding* a donut every day, I go to her office and see her sitting at her desk, just like usual.

But something's wrong.

In the morning, Miss Maria always has a box on her desk with the donut waiting. This time there's no donut. There is a box, but it's covered by a lid and it's way too big to hold a single donut. I look at her and she's not smiling at me.

"I know," she says, "you're thinking, *Where's the donut?* Well, I have something different for you today."

I don't want to be rude, so I nod and say, "Thank you,

Miss Maria." But deep inside I'm disappointed because I really like the donuts, and I'm hungry right now.

"Tani, do you remember how I was telling you that I have a son who's a year older than you?"

I nod. I do remember about her son because Miss Maria told me he is really tall and into basketball. I'd like to be tall and be able to play basketball.

"Well," says Miss Maria as she lifts the lid off the big box on her desk. "His grandma bought him these and they don't fit him." Inside I can see a pair of sneakers. They look brand new, like they've never been worn. "I thought they might fit you. Do you want to try them on?"

I don't know much about sneakers, but I like these a lot. They are the whitest pair I've ever seen, and they look like the kind of sneakers that really good basketball players wear.

So I say, "Oh, yes please, Miss Maria."

I kick my shoes off and slide my feet into the new sneakers. I've never felt a pair of shoes that are so comfortable. And when I stand up in them and try jumping, I feel like I could easily jump *ten feet* into the air.

"They look like they're a perfect fit, Tani," says Miss Maria.

I am practicing my jumping when Mom comes in and listens to Miss Maria explain about her son and his grandma and that I can have the shoes if I want. Mom says, "Thank you! You are so kind, Miss Maria," and everyone's smiling and laughing.

I don't walk to school, I *fly*! I'm like an astronaut on the moon, taking giant leaps and great big bounces.

It's a good day.

All during school I keep thinking about my new sneakers. When I walk in them, I feel like I could jump almost as high as Austin can. But then during a lesson, Miss Grant, who is probably my favorite teacher ever, starts telling a story about a woman named Rosa Parks, and it makes me stop thinking about shoes completely.

I don't remember all of her story, but I do know that Rosa Parks lived in America in a time when you were treated badly if your skin was a certain color. If you had dark skin like mine, there were some places where you weren't allowed to use the same faucets, eat in the same restaurants, or sit on the same bus seats as white people. It was as if the white people thought the others were dirty or dangerous in some way.

Anyway, Rosa Parks had dark skin, and she was tired of being treated badly. Then one day on the bus, when she was sitting in the section she was supposed to be sitting in, the driver told her to move and let a white person have her seat. But Rosa Parks didn't move. She refused to give up her seat, and she stayed on the bus. She had to be brave, especially as the police came and she got in a lot of trouble.

Because Rosa Parks stood up for herself, a lot of people started to get brave. And after a while, the laws in America about people with a certain color skin not using faucets or restaurants or bus seats were changed. And when that happened, things were made a lot more fair for everyone.

It's strange, but Rosa Parks makes me think of Miss Maria. It would have been easy for Rosa Parks to move when she was told to, but she chose to do something difficult. And because of her choice, a lot of good things happened.

It would have been easy for Miss Maria not to bring the sneakers into the office or not to buy an extra donut every single morning. But she chooses to do it anyway.

Maybe good things will happen because of her. I hope so.

CHAPTER 15

SHUSH!

It's my second week in the chess program, and I'm wearing my new *PS 116 NYC* chess T-shirt. I'm sitting at the front, listening hard to Coach Russ. But some kids are talking and I find it hard to hear, so I do something I've never done in any class before. I turn around and shush them.

Everyone stops talking. Including Coach Russ.

I turn back. Coach Russ is staring at me. I wonder if I'm in trouble. Maybe it's not polite to do shushing.

Then he smiles, nods at me, and says, "You all need to be more like Tani. He's sitting here, focused and listening and ready to work hard and do his best."

I feel kind of embarrassed. But I'm also pleased. Not because of the shushing, but because I think it's good to work hard, even though some people at school like to pretend that it's not cool.

I'm glad that I got people to be quiet because Coach Russ is talking about how great it is to live in New York City and to learn about chess.

"This city is full of chess history," he says. "And a lot of that is because of a man named Bobby Fischer."

Someone in the back of the room tries to be funny. "Was he a fisherman?" Nobody really laughs.

"Nope," says Coach Russ. "But nice try. Bobby Fischer was possibly the greatest chess player ever to have lived. His family moved to New York City when he was six years old, and they were poor. He and his sister started to learn chess, but she got bored so he had to play on his own. Bobby played a lot. He got so good that when he was thirteen years old, one of the best chess masters in the whole country came to New York to play him. Even though Bobby Fischer was half the age of the master, he won. It was such a famous game that people call it the Game of the Century."

Coach Russ continues talking, explaining how because of Bobby Fischer and other great players, chess is still really popular in the city today. "Each weekend crowds of people head to Washington Square Park and Union Square Park and other places to play chess. Almost every schoolkid is given an opportunity to learn how to play. You're in a special, special place."

I like hearing Coach Russ talk like this. I like the idea that hundreds and thousands of other people are living around me who all like to play chess. I like belonging to this special club of New York chess lovers.

Later on that day, when the chess program is almost over, it is Coach Shawn's turn to stand at the front and talk to everyone. It's getting late, and I guess that some people must be tired or hungry or whatever. Apart from Coach Shawn, everyone is silent. Everybody is listening to what he is saying. There's no need for me to do any shushing.

The reason is because he's talking about his own life.

"Chess has absolutely saved my life," Coach Shawn says. "I used to make bad decisions, even when the right decisions were in front of my face. I was skipping school, not working hard. Even when I had learned to play chess, I wasn't taking my responsibilities seriously. And one day, when I was supposed to be representing my school at a national competition, I disappeared."

Someone asks the question I'm wondering: "Where did you go?"

Coach Shawn half smiles. "I was playing Blitz on Wall Street."

I don't understand what those words mean, so I hold my hand up and ask him to explain.

"Okay, Wall Street is where the rich guys work in the city. Blitz is when your game only lasts a short time, like two or three minutes. It's fast and you've got to be your best. And if you're playing for money, there are no excuses. It'll cost you if you don't play your best."

Profile: New York City

Nickname: the Big Apple

Population: 8,550,405 (2015); it is the most populated city in the United States.

Government: The mayor is the city's top leader, but each of the five boroughs—the Bronx, Brooklyn, Manhattan, Queens, and Staten Island—have their own borough president.

Languages: There are over eight hundred languages spoken in the city. Almost half of all families in New York City speak a language other than English at home. The languages most spoken are English, Spanish, Chinese, and Russian.

Size: 305 square miles

Sports and Activities: New York hosts eight professional sports teams in baseball, basketball, football, hockey, and soccer. Basketball is a popular game to play, and many neighborhoods have their own courts. New Yorkers also love chess. There are permanent chessboards and tables in parks throughout the city, but Washington Square Park is the most famous chess park of all.

Industry: New York City is a hub for many US
businesses. Wall Street is home to the financial
industry. Many international shipping and
technology companies also call New York City
home. Tourism is one of the city's top industries;
millions of people visit the city's historic and
cultural sites, theaters, restaurants, and museums
each year.

Fast Facts

The highest point in New York City is the One World
Trade Center, which rises 1,776 feet tall.

Every 4.4 minutes a baby is born in New York City.

The first pizzeria in the United States opened in New
York City in 1905.

The Empire State Building gets hit
by lightning about twenty-three times per year.

New York City has the world's largest transportation
system, which includes over seven hundred subway
and train stations.

I nod. I kind of understand.

"Guys," says Coach Shawn, "you gotta believe us when we tell you about learning from other people. Take the advice from someone who has already made mistakes. You don't have to feel the fire for yourself to know that it's gonna burn. You don't hit your head to know if it's gonna hurt. Take the advice of your coaches and learn to make good decisions. And if you do that, Coach Russ and I guarantee you this—you won't just make good decisions at the chessboard, you'll make good decisions in life."

It's funny, but when Coach Shawn talks about making good decisions, it reminds me of Dad. It's the kind of thing he would say, although Dad wouldn't be smiling like Coach Shawn smiles when he talks. Dad likes to look serious when he's making a serious point.

When I get back to the Hotel that night, I'm glad that Dad has not yet gone to work. I want to tell him about what I've heard at the chess program today, especially what Coach Shawn said about learning from him and Coach Russ.

Dad is really tired, but he listens while I tell him everything that I can remember. And when I'm done talking, he says the word that he always says when he's truly impressed.

"Wow!" He smiles too. "These coaches of yours, Coach Russ and Coach Shawn, they are wise men, giving you good advice. I thank God for them."

"I do too," I say.

CHAPTER 16

TWO HUNDRED PUZZLES

It doesn't take long before I discover that Coach Russ is right about how much people in New York City like chess. I go down for breakfast one day, and I'm wearing my brand-new *PS 116 NYC* chess program T-shirt—the blue one where the letters are made to look like chess pieces.

"Nice T-shirt," says Jacki, the lady who works in the office. "Do you play?"

"I'm learning," I say. "I go to a program every week."

"That's good. You have a board?"

I nod. "My mom bought me one."

"If you want to play, bring it down and I'll give you a game."

I say that I'd like to, and we agree that I'll visit her later that day when I get back from school.

The elephant sits, huge and round, in my stomach throughout the day. It's only when school finishes and I'm walking home with Mom that I realize what it is. I'm nervous about Jacki and chess.

"You okay?" Mom asks me.

I tell her about Jacki and the game, and she tells me that it's a great idea.

"But what if I lose?"

Mom looks serious for a moment. "If you lose, would that make you want to give up playing forever?"

"No way!" I say.

"And if you win, would you still want to keep on playing?"

"Of course I would."

"Then winning or losing doesn't seem to matter that much, does it?"

She's right. I know it right away.

I'm still a little nervous when I walk into the office and see Jacki sitting at her desk. But she smiles and welcomes me in and tells me that she's been looking forward to our game all day.

I set the board up, and she goes first. It's strange sitting opposite Jacki. I've never played a grown-up before.

Jacki's good. A lot of the time when I play at the program, my opponents will smile when they think they're doing well or frown when they think I'm doing well. But

Jacki's face is like a statue, so I can't tell whether she's finding the game difficult or easy.

Jacki catches me by surprise and takes one of my bishops. I realize that I have not been concentrating hard enough on my moves. I've been doing something that Coach Shawn calls "hope chess." That's when you just play any move and hope it works.

Pretty soon I find out that it really doesn't work. Jacki takes a few more of my pieces—my knight, a pawn, and then the other bishop—and all I have is a couple of her pawns. She's winning, and still her face is stone. But the strange thing is that it's okay. I don't feel worried or sad or angry or anything like that.

And when she finally says "checkmate" and reaches out to shake my hand, I feel okay too. I've lost, but I don't feel bad.

I just want to go and practice a whole lot more so I can get better.

Coach Shawn and Coach Russ have given me some chess puzzles to complete during the week. I have to borrow Mom's phone to do them, but they're fun. The more I complete, the more I want to do. I don't know how many puzzles I'm supposed to be doing, so I just keep doing them for as long as Mom lets me have her phone.

At the next chess program, Coach Russ stands up and

says, "Hey, everyone, I need to talk to you about Tani and Aviel."

Aviel is older than me and he's in another class. I don't know him really, so I don't know if I should be worried or not.

But then Coach Russ smiles at me. "Now listen up," he says. "You know we keep on telling you how important it is to do your puzzles each week, right?"

"Yes, Coach Russ."

"Not all of you are doing them though, are you?"

Nobody says anything. I want to look around but decide not to.

"Every time you complete a puzzle, the site records it and adds up your weekly total. Coach Shawn and I go through them every week to see who deserves to be celebrated and who needs some encouragement to work a little harder. And I've got to tell you that last week Aviel and Tani did way more puzzles than anyone else. Some of you did 40, a couple did 50. But Tani did 112, and Aviel did almost 200. That's the kind of hard work and commitment you need if you want to succeed at this game."

Part of me is pleased that I have done well. The other part of me is trying to work out how I can beat two hundred next week.

CHAPTER 17

LION CUB

On my third week at the chess program, just when people are leaving, Coach Russ calls me over. "Hey, Tani," he says. "Is it true that you've only been playing chess for three weeks now?"

"Yes, Coach Russ."

He gives me a big smile. "You're working hard and doing really well. Are you enjoying it?"

It's my turn to smile. "Oh yes, Coach Russ. Chess is great."

Then he says something that makes me frown. "There's a tournament here on Sunday. Would you like to come and play?"

I don't know anything about tournaments, so I say, "What's that?"

"Okay," says Coach Russ, nodding. "A tournament is where a bunch of players meet up to play each other. They play three matches each, and you get one point for a win, half for a draw, and nothing if you lose. The person with the most points at the end of the day is the winner. What do you think?"

"Um," I say, looking at my feet. "Do you think I'm ready?"

"Nobody feels ready for their first tournament," says Coach Russ. "But you're working hard, and we'd love to see you on Sunday. What do you say?"

We usually go to Pastor Philip's church on Sunday, so I'm not sure, but I nod anyway.

On Sunday morning, Mom walks with me to school. As soon as we get inside and she sees Coach Russ and Coach Shawn, she starts talking and laughing with them.

I don't feel much like talking though. Or laughing. I've got elephant problems again.

I've never seen so many people ready to play chess. I hear someone say that there are 157 players. Usually when we have the after-school chess program, there are 30 or 40 kids who come along. This morning, there are more tables with chessboards than I can count. It's all so big and serious looking. The more I look, the worse my stomach feels.

Next to each chessboard is a clock that has two displays, side by side, and two big buttons on top. I've seen them at the program before, but I've never used one.

"Don't worry about that," says Coach Shawn, who is kneeling down beside me. "All you have to do is hit the button when you've played your move. And if you need help, just ask. We're here."

I feel a little less nervous for a few minutes, and I try to remember the lessons that my coaches have taught me. I remind myself that I need to think carefully about my moves and not play hope chess. I remind myself that it's good to have pieces working in pairs, and that a pair of bishops is powerful. I remind myself that even if I'm just one pawn up in a game, that's good. Even though it looks little, a pawn can be a powerful piece.

But when the tournament starts and I sit down to play my first match, I feel worse and forget about all of this. I get confused about some of the pieces and forget which one does what. Soon I'm feeling stuck, and I guess my opponent is too because a supervisor says, "That's a draw, guys."

Some people might think that it's weird to draw a game like chess, but it's really simple. If you can't win and your opponent can't win, then you can offer a draw. You get a half point for it, so in competitions it's better to draw than lose.

I also draw the second game.

Someone tells me that the players I am up against are

all beginners just like me, but that doesn't help. My head feels hot and my stomach is painful again, and I can't stop thinking about how I am not winning my matches.

While I'm waiting for my third and final game, Coach Shawn sits down next to me. He says, "Tani, do you want to know what I think about you?"

The elephant inside starts moving in a whole new way, stomping around like he's really angry. I like Coach Shawn and he's great, but there's a bit of me that is worried he might be sad that I've played two games and not won either of them. So I don't say anything and sit as still as I can.

"I think you're my lion," says Coach Shawn. "You're smart and you're hardworking and you don't miss a beat. And like a lion cub, you're learning so much right now. Even today, these last two games, you're learning. That's all you need to do. Keep trying. Keep playing. Keep learning. Do your best, remember the openings we talked about, and the winning will take care of itself."

I feel a little bit better, but I'm still nervous, especially as I hear my name called for my final match.

I sit down at the board and try to forget all about whether I'm going to win or lose or draw. Instead I think about how I want to get my pieces into the center of the board and then protect them with other pieces to make sure they are safe.

The game starts slow, but I'm trying hard to concentrate. And as the minutes go by, I forget about everything else that's going on around me, even the noise of the other players in the room. It's just me and my opponent and the chessboard and the battle that the pieces are fighting.

The guy I'm playing starts rushing his moves and makes a blunder, so I take one of his bishops. Then, just a few moves later, I nearly take his queen.

I'm getting excited and thinking about how to work out another way of taking his queen. He's using one of his knights to protect her, so I figure that all I have to do is take the knight.

TANI'S CHESS
TIP #2
Remember
openings.

I try one way first, then another. I'm concentrating so hard on the corner of the board with his queen and his knight that I don't pay any attention to what else is going on in other parts of the board.

And that's a problem. Because soon he's sitting back, looking at me, and holding out his hand. "Checkmate!" he says.

It's over.

I've lost.

CHAPTER 18

FIST BUMP

I don't like crying, but I can't stop. As soon as I find Mom, I stand next to her and hide my face in her coat. I don't want to look at anyone, and I don't want anyone to look at me.

Coach Russ comes over. "You don't need to feel bad, Tani," he says. "You're just three weeks old! Keep on trying. Next tournament you will do well. I promise."

I don't want to be rude, but I don't really want to listen either. All I want to do is leave and go back to the Hotel. But we don't leave because Mom is still talking to Coach Russ.

"Thank you," she says.

"Don't be put off by this, Mrs. Adewumi. He's doing good. He's ready to learn, and we can all see that he's a really great guy. We love having him around. This is just the start."

All the way back to the Hotel I don't want to think about chess or playing in any other tournaments ever again. But the next morning I feel better. I don't think I want to play in a match anytime soon, but I start doing puzzles again. And by the time I get to Thursday afternoon and school ends, I put on my *PS 116 NYC* chess T-shirt. I'm ready and excited to go to the chess program.

And do you know what happens?

When Coach Shawn stands up to announce who has completed the most puzzles that week, it's not Aviel or any other kid. It's me! I've completed more than three hundred puzzles, more than anyone else.

I'm amazed and super pleased, and it totally makes me forget all about losing my last game.

I wait for the moment when everyone starts doing their practice so I can ask Coach Shawn the question that's been growing inside me since the tournament.

If you look up a chess player, you will see a number next to their name. That's their rating, or how many points they've earned in competition. A player's rating tells you how good they are. The very best players in my school are maybe at 1600, and grand masters (the absolute best players in the world) have ratings of over 2500.

I don't have a rating, or I didn't until Sunday. Taking

part in my first tournament means that my scores have been recorded officially, and I have an actual rating.

"Coach Shawn," I say when he visits me at my table. "Can you check my rating please?"

He pulls out his phone and looks hard at the screen. Then he nods and shows me the page with my name, my school, and my rating.

"One hundred and five," I say.

Coach Shawn gets down on his knees beside me. "You okay with that, my lion?"

I think for a moment. One hundred and five is low. It's really low. In fact, it's probably the lowest score you could possibly get. But even though I'm thinking this, I don't feel bad. I don't feel like I did when I lost that last game.

"Coach Shawn," I say, "I think I am okay with it. I think it means that I can improve."

He smiles and gives me a fist bump. "That's right. You can't get lower. There's only one way you can go now, Tani."

CHAPTER 19

FLYING

I'm not so sure how I feel about tournaments, but I like doing puzzles. In the weeks after I get my rating, I decide that I'm going to spend as much time as I possibly can using Mom's phone and completing puzzles.

Some weeks I complete four hundred or even five hundred puzzles. Sometimes Aviel has done more, sometimes not. And sometimes other kids in the chess program have done more than me. That's okay though. I like being in a program where lots and lots of people want to work hard and get better.

I also keep playing Jacki in the office, and sometimes I even win. Other people work in the Hotel too, and they let me play. Sometimes they win. Sometimes I win.

And still I want to play more.

And more.

And more.

So when Coach Shawn invites me to enroll in a chess club he runs every Saturday morning, straight away I say to him, "Yes please, Coach Shawn!"

I ask Mom, and even though it's in Harlem, which is a long, long way from the Hotel, she says yes. She's the best mom ever.

Saturday chess club is great. I get to spend three whole hours playing chess. I also get to meet some new kids, and all of them love chess like I do. I can tell that they're all doing deep thinking. I watch them all, and I figure out that deep thinking doesn't always look the same on everyone. A lot of people go still as statues and stare at the board like it's about to burst into fire. Others stare up at the ceiling as if they are looking for a spider hiding up in the corner.

The puzzles and the games and the chess club all make me super happy. Sometimes they make me so happy that I can feel all this excitement bumping around inside me.

It happens one Sunday morning when we're all going to church. Dad is wearing one of his best suits, Mom is dressed in a pretty, brightly colored dress, and Austin and I are both wearing clean white shirts and shoes so polished I can almost see my reflection in them.

We ride the elevator down to the street and walk out through the spinning doors. It's cold, but that's okay. I do what I often do and run down the sidewalk to the end of the block. I love running like this, especially early on Sunday mornings when the sidewalks are almost empty.

It doesn't take me long to reach the end, and I stop like I'm a car that's slammed on my brakes. "Come on!" I shout back, laughing to the others. "If you run, you won't feel the cold so much."

Austin can run, but it's too early for him, so I know he won't. Mom and Dad . . . well, they don't run often, and they *never* run when they're dressed up for church.

So I'm left bouncing on the corner, looking up at the buildings that are towering above me.

And then it happens.

I see a particular building. Ever since we moved into the Hotel, this building has been covered up because workers have been fixing it. Well, the workers must have finished because for the first time, the building is not hidden. It's being unwrapped like a Christmas present, and we can finally see what it looks like beneath.

"Wow!" says Dad.

It's the shiniest building in the whole city. It looks like a gigantic mirror, and I can't stop staring at it.

"Come on, Tani," says Austin as the lights turn green and they cross the street. "Let's go."

But I don't move.

I'm thinking about all the good things that have happened to us since we moved to New York: Pastor Philip, the Hotel, Miss Maria and Jacki, PS 116 and Coach Shawn and Coach Russ. Austin is doing well in his school, Mom is able to cook, and Dad has a job. There are so many kind people around us, and life is really, really good.

All these things pile up on me. Together they feel like another miracle.

When we lived in Dallas, life wasn't good. And when we left, even though I believed Dad when he said that our new life in America was finally about to begin, I didn't dream it would be *this good*.

But it is. Life. Is. Good.

I'm grateful for all the good things and all the kind people. And I'm grateful to God too. He's kind and He's super great at looking after people and helping them.

And then I have this idea. Or is it a hope? Maybe it's a prayer or something else completely. Whatever it is, I can feel it growing inside me.

"What is it, Son?" says Dad.

The idea is getting bigger and bigger. Soon it's too big to hold inside.

"We've been helped so much. Maybe we can help others. Maybe one day, if God allows it, we will build a very tall building just like that one there. And we will live on top of it, and all the other floors we will make into a shelter just like the Hotel so that other people who need a home but don't have one can come and live with us."

Dad looks at me. His eyes are strong, his face is serious. "Amen!" he says with a voice that's even deeper and louder than the sound of the traffic.

Austin and Mom start saying it too. "Amen! Amen!"

And that's when I start running again. I'm flying toward the subway entrance as fast as I've ever run in my life. It's like there's a hurricane inside of me, pushing me on. For a moment, I don't think I'll ever get tired.

CHAPTER 20

THE ANSWER IS
ON THE BOARD

I was only three weeks old as a chess player when I took part in my first tournament. That's pretty young.

Now I'm two months old as a chess player. I'm still young, but I'm about to go to my second tournament. I've done a lot of puzzles, and I've been to a lot of chess programs, and you know what? I still feel nervous.

The tournament isn't at PS 116. It's at a different school in the city, and this time there are even more tables with chessboards because there are even more people playing. It's loud. Everywhere you go, there are people, and I don't recognize any of them.

But Coach Shawn has warned me about this, so I try as hard as I can not to let my mind be distracted or to think about how I have this funny feeling inside my stomach.

TANI'S CHESS
TIP #3
Practice with
chess puzzles.

Instead I think about puzzles.

Chess puzzles are so much fun, and there are lots of different kinds you can do. Of all the challenges, my favorites are the ones where you have to get to checkmate in a certain number of moves. I love starting a puzzle like this because I know that the answer is on the board. All I have to do is concentrate real hard and search until I find it.

So I'm thinking about puzzles while I wait for my first match to begin. I'm thinking about how I like to start a game and how I like to end it, and I'm trying to remember what the board should look like when everything's going well for me.

Even though I don't know many people here, there are three other kids from the chess program at PS 116. We're all standing near each other in a corner of the hall when Coach Shawn calls us in.

"Okay," he says, "gather round in a circle. I want to talk to you."

We stand in close and Coach Shawn bends down so his head is level with ours. He looks at each of us, right in the eyes. He talks quietly, so we all have to lean in to hear.

"You're all my lions," he says. "You've all worked hard, and I believe that all of you can do your best today.

And if you do that, we'll all be so proud of you, whatever the result."

The first game is over really, really quickly. I get my pawns and my knights into the place where I like them to be, and I'm just trying to get my bishops out, when my opponent makes a massive blunder. He moves a pawn that was protecting his king, and I look at the board and it feels just like a puzzle. I *know* that I can get checkmate from here. And I do!

The second game is totally different. It's tough because I play against a boy who is super good *and* who plays super fast. At first it bothers me, and I get distracted and think about what it would be like to play Blitz. But then I tell myself to stop thinking about that and concentrate on the game and nothing else. When I do that, I win.

Then the third match starts. It's a strange game because my opponent keeps looking over at his coach. He's nervous, but I tell myself not to worry about that. I focus on controlling the pieces the way I want to control them.

And I win!

After I've shaken hands with my opponent, I go back to the corner of the hall where Mom and Coach Shawn and the others from PS 116 are waiting. They're all looking at me, so I do something I saw another kid do at my first tournament. I make my face go all soft and still so that nobody can guess whether I have won or lost. Then I stick my arm out in front of me. My hand is in a fist. Slowly I let my thumb poke out to the side. Then I point it straight up, showing them that I've won.

"Wow!" says Coach Shawn. He gives me a massive high five that's so hard my hand stings. But I don't mind. "You've only been playing for two months and you've just gone three and o! That's so great, Tani!"

Even Coach Russ is here, and he says, "Tani, I'm so proud of how hard you're working."

And Mom gives me a big hug that lasts forever.

But do you want to know what I like best about it all?

After we've been waiting for a while longer and the last matches have finished, all the players who have won all their matches like I did get invited up to shake hands with the people that organized the event. And do you know what they give me?

A trophy!

It's about as tall as a magazine, not too heavy, and has a little gold sign on it that says, "Under 300 Section, 1st Place." It sparkles and shines, and I think it's the coolest thing ever.

I pick it up and hold it close. I'm never letting it go!

CHAPTER 21

MEETING FABIANO

Winning my first tournament changes my ranking. It goes from 105 all the way up to 365! But 365 isn't that high really, and lots and lots of other kids in PS 116 have higher ratings than me.

So I decide that I should just keep doing the same things I have been doing. I do as many puzzles as I can each week. If Austin wants to play, I play with him. And if Jacki or anyone else at the Hotel has the time, I play them as well. I make sure that I'm always sitting at the front and listening to everything the coaches say at the Thursday chess program. I do the same on Saturday mornings at the chess club in Harlem.

For a few weeks after I win my first tournament, I look at the trophy in my bedroom and wonder when I'm going to win another one. It turns out that I don't have to wait long. Only, the second time I get a trophy, I don't actually win it. But I learn a good lesson all the same.

Let me explain . . .

My third tournament is one that Coach Russ has organized. I play okay, but because my rating is now above 300, I'm playing against players who are much better. I don't win every game, but I do well enough to finish in eleventh place.

At the end of the day, Coach Russ announces who won each age group. Everyone is standing around, and I'm looking at the table that has all the trophies. As Coach Russ calls out all the players who finished in places one through ten, he hands each of them a trophy. I watch the winning players with their trophies and their smiles, and I wish I could have done better and gotten myself a trophy.

"What's up?" says Coach Russ. "You're not happy, Tani? I thought you played well today. These players are a lot tougher than the last kids you played against."

I shrug. "I wanted a trophy."

Coach Russ smiles, then says, "Wait there." He disappears out a back door and I wait. I wait a long time.

When he comes back, he's holding a trophy and a pen. I watch him write something on the trophy. Then he hands it to me. It says "Tani—Most Improved Player. Never Stop and Never Ask for a Trophy Again."

I'm not sure if this is a good thing or not, so I look back at Coach Russ. He's smiling at me.

I decide right there and right then that I will never *ever* ask for another trophy. If I am going to get any more, I'm going to win them myself.

There's only just enough space on the dresser in the Hotel for me to put the trophy that Coach Russ gave me next to the one I won at my second tournament. I like that it says I'm an improved player, but I like more that it reminds me to always work hard.

And that's what I do. I do more puzzles. I learn different openings. I do everything that Coach Shawn and Coach Russ suggest. And when Mom lets me, I watch lots and lots of YouTube videos about chess. And that's how I hear about Fabiano.

Fabiano Caruana is the number-two chess player in the world. He became a grand master—which is the best level you can get to—when he was only *fourteen years old*! And guess where he grew up? That's right. He grew up in Brooklyn, right here in New York City.

I watch *so many* videos of Fabiano. He's amazing. He's won almost everything that you can win, and he's so cool. But this is the best bit. One day, maybe two months after I won my first trophy, Coach Shawn asks me and

Aviel and another kid named Lilly to stay behind after club on Thursday.

"There's a charity chess event next week, where people pay money to play grand masters. Fabiano is going to be there, and I've been given tickets to go and watch. Would you three lions like to come along?"

I almost can't speak I'm so excited. And the night before the charity chess event, I can't get to sleep. On the actual day that Mom and I arrive at the address Coach Shawn gave us, I'm so excited I'm almost shaking.

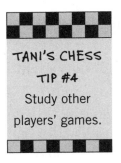

TANI'S CHESS
TIP #4
Study other players' games.

It looks kind of like a tournament. There are lots of boards laid out and people getting ready to play. But it doesn't look much like either of the two tournaments I've been to. Instead of kids wearing their school chess T-shirts, there are lots and lots of adults standing around wearing suits. And instead of plastic tables and chairs, the furniture is made of wood and glass, and you can see almost the entire city from the windows. I like it here, but it would be easy to get distracted by everything there is to look at.

That doesn't matter to me, though, because I'm not here to play. I'm just here to watch. Coach Shawn has told me that twenty grand masters are going to be in the room, and I recognize some of them from the videos I've watched. They are all smiling and look totally normal, which surprises me. I thought that maybe they would be taller or more serious or they would look different from other people.

But what is even more amazing than seeing all these great chess players is that when Mom and I see Coach Shawn and go over to say hi to him, he says, "Do you want to come and meet Fabiano?"

I can't believe what he just said. "Do you know him?"

"Sure." He laughs. "He's from Brooklyn, remember?"

"Coach Shawn, do you think he'll talk to me?"

He frowns and looks confused. "Are you kidding? He'd love to."

Mom and I follow Coach Shawn as he walks over to a crowd of people. I'm feeling really nervous, like ten times worse than I felt when I played my first tournament. Everyone is so tall, and I feel small. I almost wish I hadn't said that I'd like to meet Fabiano.

Just when I'm wondering if maybe Mom and I should go back, Coach Shawn steps aside and suddenly Fabiano is standing *right in front of me*! He holds out his hand for me to shake and says, "It's nice to meet you, Tani."

I shake his hand, but I don't know what to say. My mouth has forgotten how to speak.

Coach Shawn is smiling and takes a photo of Fabiano and me standing together. When he's finished with the photo, he says, "You gotta watch this kid, Fabiano. I'm telling you, he's good. He's been playing four months, and he's already winning tournaments."

I *still* don't know what to say, but Fabiano laughs. And I'm smiling the biggest smile I've ever smiled in my life.

Hours later, when I'm tired and it's dark outside and I get into bed, I'm still smiling. I'll probably still be smiling when I wake up.

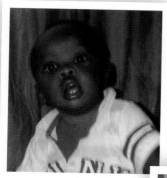

Me in Abuja in 2011. My parents say that even as a baby, I was always fascinated by the world around me.

Two happy brothers on a trip to Ado Ekiti to visit family in 2011

Austin and me at home in Abuja. Even back in 2012, our personalities shone through.

Keeping it real on the streets of Abuja in 2014

Our home in Abuja in 2016, not long before our family came to the attention of Boko Haram

Happy and safe—though a little cold!— in the USA

Coach Russ and me sharing a special moment while crossing Third Avenue outside of PS 116 in Midtown East, New York City

World No. 2 Grandmaster Fabiano Caruana versus *me* in St. Louis, Missouri, at a private event during the 2019 US Championship

Competing at G & T Saturday quads held at PS 111 in New York City

Me with my first place trophy after winning the 2019 K–3 New York State Championship in Saratoga Springs

Coach Shawn and me with my K–3
New York State Championship trophy

Coach Russ celebrating with me
after finding out I clinched the K–3
New York State Championship

The March 23, 2019, headline in the
New York Times piece said it all: "Our
Chess Champion Has a Home."

CHRISTOPHER LEE / *The New York Times*

Coach Russ (far right), Coach Shawn
(far left), me, and the cast from the
Today show after appearing on live TV

Playing chess on the set
of the *Today* show

Coach Shawn and me at the 2019 United States Chess Federation National Elementary Championship held in Nashville, Tennessee

Me at the Elementary Nationals

Rated match play hosted at the 2019 G & T Summer Training Camp held at PS 33 in New York City

Coach Shawn, Coach Russ, Coach Angel, and my family outside of the World Chess Hall of Fame in St. Louis, Missouri

Once President Clinton and I started talking about the people we admire, nobody else could get a word in!

Me and my parents with Coach Russ and Coach Shawn. Words cannot express how grateful our family is for these two men.

So much has changed for our family in recent years. But the love that holds us together remains the same.

CHAPTER 22

MALALA'S COURAGE

Sometime after I meet Fabiano, Miss Grant holds up a book that she's just finished reading.

"It's a true story about a girl named Malala Yousafzai," she says. Some boys in the class stop listening, but not me. I like true stories, and I don't mind if they're about a girl or a boy. And everything Miss Grant says about this book makes me want to read it.

"This girl lived a long way from here in a country called Pakistan. When some bad people moved into the area, they made some new rules that made life hard for people. They said that music was a crime and that women couldn't go to the market anymore. But the worst rule of all for Malala was the one that said girls couldn't go to school."

Some of the boys are listening again, and they laugh about not having to go to school.

"I know," says Miss Grant. "That doesn't sound too bad, does it? But right from when she was a little kid, Malala was taught to stand up for what she believed in. And she believed that going to school is important. So she decided to stand up to the bad guys and fight for her right to get an education."

I look closely at the cover of the book. The girl doesn't look like much of a fighter. She looks ordinary. She looks like a chess player. I like that.

"One day, Malala was riding the bus back from school when some of those bad men got on the bus and shot her."

Silence fills the classroom. Everybody's listening now.

"Malala survived," Miss Grant says. "But she didn't stay silent. She continued telling people that girls should be allowed to go to school."

The bell rings. It's time for recess and everyone hurries out. But not me.

"Miss Grant," I say. "Can I borrow that book, please? I'd like to read it."

I like reading a lot. Every night when I go to bed, I read a book. Most nights the book falls onto my face when I fall asleep.

But when I'm reading the book about this girl, I don't

feel much like sleeping. I read page after page, and I can't stop until I've finished the whole book.

I admire Malala a lot. Her passion is so great. And because of what she did, girls are able to go to school in Pakistan today.

Something else about her story stays in my head long after I've finished it. Whenever I think about her story, I end up remembering what happened to my family, and in a way, it's similar. Bad people tried to take over in Abuja, but Dad stood up to them. Kind of like Malala. And when it looked like the bad guys were going to win, Dad didn't give up. Just like Malala.

And here's one more thing. Malala's story doesn't end with her recovering from being shot. She went on to tell her story to people all over the world, reminding them how important it is for *everyone* to be able to go to school.

When you don't give up, good things can happen.

CHAPTER 23

PAUL MORPHY'S QUEEN

When I first hear about the summer camp that Coach Russ organizes, I'm excited. I've never been to a summer camp before, and I *really* like the idea of spending eight hours a day practicing chess. But when school ends and the camp finally begins, it's even better than I imagined.

The camp is in a school on the other side of the city, and I have to take the subway there every day. It looks a little like PS 116, but what happens inside is a whole lot different.

At summer camp, everyone is there for one thing: to play chess. There are so many different people at camp, and some of them are *really* good at chess. Some even have ratings as high as 1600 and are state champions. I think one of them is even number two or three in the whole country for her age group. And they're all so nice and let me play them, even though I don't win very often.

I also like the other coaches I meet. They're all super friendly, especially Coach Angel. He moves slowly and his voice is gentle. I think that's why Coach Shawn says they are such good friends. He says, "Brothers couldn't be closer."

One of the best things about camp is that Coach Russ invited Austin to come and help out. Austin and I ride the subway together each morning, which is fun. It also means that Austin starts playing chess properly and improving. Soon, Austin is good enough for us to play Bughouse together.

Bughouse is an awesome way to play chess. In Bughouse, you play with a partner as a team against another pair. You sit next to each other and both play your games at the same time, but any time you capture one of your opponent's pieces, you give it to your partner who can then put it on their board and use it.

When you play Bughouse, you're allowed to give your partner advice, but Austin doesn't need a lot of help. We win our first game quickly, then the next one and the next one after that. Soon we're five and o, and we win the whole tournament! There isn't a trophy but that's okay. Winning with my brother feels good, and I do a superfast dance to celebrate.

But the best thing about summer camp is my rating. All the time practicing and playing Bughouse and learning from other coaches and players means that in just two months, my rating doubles from 550 to 1100.

Chess Player Ratings

As soon as you enter the world of chess, you're going to hear a lot about ratings. Players get a rating by competing against other players in registered tournaments. In the United States chess clubs use the Elo rating system. Beginners usually have ratings around 1200, while Experts have ratings between 2000 and 2199. Masters rate between 2200 and 2399, while International Masters rate between 2400 and 2499. The very best players, Grand masters, have ratings of 2500 or more.

It's easy to get obsessed about your rating, but don't take it too seriously. Chess is a great game that will help you in all kinds of ways, but it's still a game.

Right at the very end of camp, Coach Shawn invites me to go on a trip to somewhere he calls the Hamptons. I have to get up super early and say goodbye to Mom at Penn Station and then sit on a train for a long, long time, but it's worth it. It's like a one-day summer camp where everyone learns about chess during the day, and then right at the end, we get to play a match.

I get to play a boy who is one year older than me but who has been playing for a long time. And his rating is even higher than 1300.

I win.

When I finish shaking his hand and walk back to where my friends and coaches are, Coach Shawn asks me to sit down awhile.

"Tani, what do you think about that game?"

"Well," I say, "I won, so that was good. Wasn't it?"

He shakes his head, and I'm confused. "No, you didn't just win, Tani. You destroyed him. You were tactical, you played aggressively, you were smart and controlled and disciplined. That was . . . I don't know what it was, but I was sitting there watching, and I just kept on saying to myself, 'Wow!'"

Other games are still going on, so Coach Shawn and I play a game. He's a chess master with a rating of something like 2200, so he wins. But he must have to concentrate because at some points in the match, he goes still and his eyes stare hard at the board.

After we finish playing, I set up the board again. "Coach Shawn," I say, "I want to show you something."

I start playing both the white and the black pieces. I know exactly which pieces I want to move and where I want them to go, and as I play, I feel happy because the patterns on the board are right.

"I know this game!" says Coach Shawn. I don't say anything back because I am too busy concentrating.

"That's right, Tani. You remember what comes next?"

I nod and play on. Black is looking strong, but White is clever. White has laid a trap by sacrificing a load of pieces, and Black's king is exposed and weak. I play the last few moves and then it's over. White wins.

Coach Shawn gives me a fist bump. "Paul Morphy, huh?"

If you don't play chess, you probably have never heard of Paul Morphy. But if you do play chess, then you will *definitely* have heard of him. Paul Morphy was one of the greatest chess players ever. He was the first unofficial world champion. As soon as I'd heard some of the coaches talking about him during summer camp, I liked him.

Paul Morphy was from New Orleans, Louisiana, and he lived so long ago that there was no such thing as electricity and there were still slaves near where he lived. His dad played in the kitchen every Sunday, and Paul would watch him. One day when he was eight years old, Paul asked his dad if he could play him. His dad didn't want to because he'd never taught Paul how to play, but Paul really wanted to do it. So they played. And Paul Morphy won.

His dad was impressed and took him to his chess club. Paul won there too. And the more he played, the better he got. He got so good that he became one of the best players in the whole world. He might even have been the actual best player, but this was such a long time ago that the official organization of chess hadn't been set up yet, so there was nobody organizing world championship matches. But if there had been a championship and Paul Morphy had played, he probably would have won.

Coach Shawn had told me all about Paul Morphy. He told me how most other players at the time played slowly, but Paul played fast and aggressive and won games in as few as twenty moves. That's *quick*.

Even though Paul Morphy was alive a long time ago, he still did what every chess player does today and recorded the moves he made in each match in a notebook. So you can look up hundreds of his games online and see for yourself how great a player he was.

I like looking at Paul Morphy's matches. I like the way that he laid traps and controlled the center of the board. I like the way that he sacrificed pieces so he could win. One of his most famous games is called the Opera Game because he was playing two opponents while an actual opera show was going on. In the Opera Game, he sacrificed his queen so that he could win.

When I started playing chess, I didn't like losing pieces. But the more I play, the more I think that sometimes it's not so bad after all.

Sometimes you have to sacrifice a piece if you want to win.

CHAPTER 24

YOU ONLY
EVER WIN

Coach Russ is so kind. In addition to letting me join the chess program and summer camp, even though we couldn't afford the fees, he also lets me go along to lots of tournaments. And when winter approaches and we've almost been living in New York for one whole year, he even pays for Mom and me to fly to Orlando, Florida, to take part in a big tournament.

I've been to some big tournaments before, but this one is *really* big. It's in a hotel, and everywhere you look are kids and parents and coaches. It's so big there's even a shop where you can buy things like chess books and clocks and a whole bunch of other stuff.

I look in the shop, but all the items are expensive, so I don't go back. Instead, if I'm not playing a match, I spend all my time in the team room. It's the place where all the kids and parents who attend Coach Russ's chess programs can hang out. There are lots of tables and chairs, and there's a thick brown carpet that has all different patterns on it. All my teammates from PS 116, like Aviel and Lilly, are there as well as others I know already from summer camp and other tournaments.

I like it in the team room. It's nice in here because even though you compete on your own at chess, it's good to be a part of a team. When someone wins, we all cheer. And when someone loses, we help them feel better. One of my favorite moments in the team room is when a new round of matches is just about to start and Coach Shawn calls all of us PS 116 players together.

"To be a champion you need to have the mind-set of a champion," he says. "Remember what the grand master Magnus Carlsen said when the journalist asked him if he was going to win the tournament?"

All five of us answer at the same time, chanting the words as loud as we can. "'I'm not worried about winning. I'm worried about playing my best!'"

"That's right. Now, I've got something for you all." Coach Shawn digs around in his backpack and pulls out a handful of chess pieces. They're all knights. "You're the Knights of the Round Table, remember? You've all been working so hard, and I know for sure that right now you're ready to go into battle. You're ready to do your absolute best."

I nod. Everyone nods.

"Good," says Coach Shawn, checking the time. "We're ready to go. Who's feeling confident?"

We all hold our hands up high in the air.

"All right, all right! So let's bring up the confidence meter."

We all know exactly what to do. We put our hands in the middle, down low at first, then bring them up together, cheering louder and louder as our pile of hands goes higher.

"Okay, okay, last thing now. We've got to build each of you up before we send you into battle in there. Who wants in first? Tani? Okay, come right in here. What do we say, everyone?"

I move into the middle of the circle. "Taa-ni! Taa-ni! Taa-ni!" The chanting is super loud, but nobody minds. The other kids in the team room are all smiling and laughing. We're a team, even if we come from different schools.

I win my first match, but I'm not happy about it. I played badly.

"Look at this, Tani," says Coach Shawn as we review the match in my notebook. He's pointing to the part of the game where I realized that I could win, and I moved my bishop to prepare the attack. "This is what I'm talking about. You make moves of such quality; they're so confident and bold."

"Yeah, but I could have lost. I blundered."

"True, but you didn't lose. And you know where you blundered, don't you?"

I can see it. "Moving my bishop like that left my queen vulnerable." It was a bad move, and I was lucky my opponent didn't see it.

"That's right. You blundered, but you saw it. And let's turn it into a positive and ask, what did you learn from this?"

It's a good question and it makes me think. "I need to not rush."

Coach Shawn gives me a fist bump. "There you go. That's a lesson right there. And it's a lesson that can take years to learn fully. But today you've got a jump on the other guys who haven't even started to figure it out."

I sigh because my stomach suddenly doesn't feel so good. "But I've got six more rounds to go. What if I blunder again?"

TANI'S CHESS
TIP #5
Don't rush.

"You just take it one round at a time. Let's not focus on a prize. Let's focus on the work, okay?"

"Yes, Coach Shawn."

"All right. So you've got a couple of

hours before your next game, and I want you to look at your openings and do another twenty puzzles. That okay?"

"That's okay," I say.

"Good. I want you to keep calm, keep your mind engaged on the game, and don't allow yourself to get distracted. Can you do that, Tani?"

"Yes, Coach Shawn."

Every other tournament I've played in has seemed big, but this one in Orlando is really big. If you take your eyes off the board, all you see are people. With so many of them playing in the hall and finishing their matches at different times, it's noisy in here. And some of the people I play against are super good. They make their moves really fast and look like they know exactly what they're doing all the time. There are *a lot* of distractions.

I think this is why I end up with three wins, one draw, and three losses. I end up in ninety-fourth place. Some of the other kids in the team room finish a lot higher than me, but they've been playing a lot longer than I have.

Just when I have finished my last match, Coach Russ finds me and asks how I'm doing. I don't feel sad, but I don't feel happy either. So I say, "I'm fine."

He nods. "You know, this tournament is a big step up for you. You've been up against kids who've been coached for years. Kids from families with no limits to their resources. Kids who spend their whole year traveling around the country to attend events like this. I don't think winning means you have to finish high enough to get a trophy. Do you understand what I mean?"

"I think so." Inside of me there's a smile that wants to come out, but there's a frown too. It's like they've got each other in check.

"You've got a lot of heart. You work hard, you're not scared of the challenges that you face, and you've got talent. But there are a ton of other kids like that. The difference between them and champions is how they handle the pressure. And I've been watching you all through the tournament, and you've handled it so well."

"But I blundered. And I lost three matches." I don't like losing as many matches as I win—that feels like a draw, not a win.

He smiles and shakes his head. "I know. But you only lose if you don't learn from a defeat. Do you feel like you've learned something here?"

I nod. "Oh yes, Coach Russ. I've learned *lots*. Don't get distracted. Keep your focus. Don't rush. Play your own game."

I'm sitting around the team room waiting for the last games to finish when some of my friends visit the shop. They come back and show me what they've bought, and

I definitely like seeing their digital clocks and limited-edition chess sets and books signed by grand masters. But I also don't want to look too long at what they show me because if I do, then I start to feel kind of weird inside, like all the lights are about to go out inside of me.

Coach Shawn has been sitting with me, but he leaves when everyone starts coming over to show me their things. I wonder if maybe he doesn't have much money either.

But then he comes back into the team room. He has a shop bag just like everyone else. "Hey, Tani. Come here, will you?"

I go to the corner of the room where he is standing. I want to be polite and happy for whatever cool thing Coach Shawn just bought himself. But then he says, "I got an early Christmas gift for you." He's holding out the bag so I can see inside.

It's a chess bag. But it isn't just a regular chess bag. It's the best chess bag I've ever seen in my *entire life*. It's black and made of leather. It has a shoulder strap as well as two handles. It has a rolled-up board inside and all the pieces as well as space for a clock and a notation book and pens. It's amazing and the best present I've ever been given—*ever*.

TANI'S CHESS
TIP #6
Learn from
your mistakes.

I jump up on a chair and give Coach Shawn a hug. I don't want to let go. But then I do let go because I want to check out my bag some more.

Then Coach Angel and Mom both come over, and I show them the bag. I put it on my back and walk around with it and everyone is saying, "Tani! Great bag!" or "Tani, you look so professional!" And I'm grinning so much my face hurts.

Then Coach Angel comes back with something from the shop. He says, "You can't have a great bag like that and not have a clock. Here, Merry Christmas!" And he gives me this amazing digital clock that fits perfectly in my bag. And then another coach who I don't even know as well as Coach Shawn or Coach Angel comes over and gives me a new notation book that he's just bought for me. I'm laughing and saying thank you and laughing some more. Mom is laughing too, but she's crying as well because that's the kind of thing moms do at times like this.

That night, I can't get to sleep. I'm thinking about my bag and my clock and my book. I'm thinking about the other kids and their shop bags and how the coaches just gave me these great gifts. It feels unbelievable and impossible. It feels like another miracle.

But that's not the only reason I'm awake. I'm also thinking about Paul Morphy sacrificing his queen to win the Opera Game. I'm thinking about Malala getting shot but not giving up. And I keep remembering what Coach Russ said: you only lose when you don't learn.

And even though it's late and I'm tired and all these thoughts are swirling around my head, keeping me awake, I've just realized something *really* important.

When you lose a match, you don't have to *lose*. If you learn from what happened, then you've gained something. So if you have the right way of thinking, you never really lose. You only ever win.

CHAPTER 25

SOMETHING BIG IS GOING TO HAPPEN

It's a gray, cold morning when Mom and I leave the Hotel and walk to PS 116. We're going on a long drive, and it reminds me of the day we took the bus from Dallas to New York. On that long and dark drive away from Grandma's house, I was unsure about what was going to happen when the bus stopped and we reached the end of the journey.

There's a part of me that feels the same way now. I know that at the end of the bus ride something big is going to happen. But when we left Dallas I was nervous. Today I'm feeling something different.

I'm happy!

As soon as Mom and I get to school, I can see my favorite people all waiting for us. Coach Russ is there and so are Coach Shawn and Coach Angel. There are two other coaches I know from the summer camp, Coach Logan and Coach Joel, and my friend Zixi is there too. As soon as Coach Aaron drives up in the white van he's rented, we all climb in. Mom's at the back, and in just a few minutes she's laughing with some of the coaches. It seems like she's part of the team, and that makes me extra happy.

I like being with these people. They're fun. But they're not the only reason I'm enjoying the ride. I'm excited. Maybe nervous as well. Why? Because we're on our way to something very, very special.

We're driving to the state championship!

I'm sitting right behind Coach Shawn, so when he pulls out his phone and starts playing a match online, I lean forward and watch. It's a live game and I know that he's concentrating, so I try not to talk and to just let him play. But Coach Shawn says that he likes me asking questions, and he has never told me to stop, so after two moves I've got all these questions inside me, and if I don't ask them I think I might burst.

"Who are you playing, Coach Shawn?"

"Why did you make that first move?"

"Is that a new opening? What's it called?"

"What rating is the person you're playing?"

"Do you think they're a master like you?"

Coach Shawn answers nearly all of my questions, but then I ask, "Did you ever play Fabiano? What happened?"

"Don't you want to take a nap, kid?" he says.

I'm wide-awake excited, and so I say, "No, Coach Shawn! I'm not at all tired."

When we finally stop driving and arrive at the rented house where we're all going to stay, I'm beginning to feel tired. But when Coach Russ shows Mom and me inside and says that because Mom is the guest of honor we get the biggest room, I don't feel tired at all. It's a *really* big room. You could put four of the rooms from the Hotel into this one room.

Mom's tired, so I go downstairs because I can hear that all the coaches are there. They are sitting around, playing chess, and laughing. I want to stay up and play with them.

"*Pleeeeeeeease*, Coach Shawn!" I beg him to let me stay up. But he shakes his head, and I know he won't let me.

"You want to do well in this tournament, Tani?"

I nod. "Yes, Coach Shawn."

"Then you'd better get to sleep."

I don't argue at all. I go straight to bed.

CHAPTER 26

STATE CHAMPIONSHIP

As soon as we get inside the team room on the first day of the state championship, even before I've taken off my chess bag and unpacked my notebook, Coach Shawn calls me and Zixi over. The room is busy already, so he tells us to lean in so we can hear him.

"Imagine I take you out from this room and magically drop you off in France," Coach Shawn says.

I look at Zixi. He's smiling just like me. I love it when Coach Shawn says crazy things like this. He always knows how to make us stop and listen and then think really hard about something.

"You're in France and you don't have a cell phone," says Coach Shawn. "You don't have a map and you can't speak the language. What's the one word that best describes how you feel?"

Zixi and I both call out at exactly the same time. "Lost!"

"That's right. And it's exactly the same with chess. You might have spent hours and hours studying your openings and remembering the moves you want to make, but if you deviate from your plan and move pieces without thinking just because you want to hurry things along and get the game finished, it's like landing in another country with no tools to help you. You'll feel lost, and it will all be because you stopped thinking and started rushing. So today I want you to do one simple thing for me. Remember your plan. Stick to it. Don't get lost."

When he's done talking, I find a corner of the room, take my notebook out of my chess bag, and sit down and remind myself of my openings. I know them already. I know them so well that I can see them all in my head, but I still read through my notes. It's how I help my brain get ready to play.

Chess is tough. Thinking about your openings and planning what you will do for every possible move that your opponent might make is *hard work*. Chess is not supposed to be an easy game to play. It's *meant* to be difficult.

I've heard some people complain about how hard they find chess. Do you know what I think? I think that if you complain and tell yourself that it's too hard, then you're going to hate the game and not want to play anymore.

But if you expect it to be hard and if you make up your mind that you won't give up easily, you're going to enjoy chess a lot more. And when you work hard like this and do your practice and play your matches, you will always have fun.

I notice something moving in front of me. I look up and see Coach Shawn.

"It's time, Tani," he says. "Are you ready?"

I don't know why I like playing fast, but I do. I really do. My coaches say that I play aggressive, and I like it when my moves take control of a game. Maybe it's because I like the way Paul Morphy played.

I also like to move my pieces quickly. Some players carefully pick up a piece, then slowly lift it off the board and hold it in the air while they wait for a long time until they carefully put it down. That's not me. I grab the piece I'm going to move and put it down as fast as I can. Then I slap the clock so that I use up as little of my time as possible.

Coach Russ doesn't like it when I do this. He especially doesn't like it when I move so fast that I don't put a piece right in the middle of the square or I even knock something over. He says that I should slow down and respect the board and pieces more.

So in the first match of the state championship, I try

super hard to do both these things. I try to keep on being aggressive and take control of the game, but I also try to slow myself down and make my hands gentle and careful whenever I'm moving a piece. It's hard.

But I breathe nice and slow and keep myself calm and remember that I really, *really* don't want to end up lost in France. I remember my opening, and move by move, I see the board take on the patterns I want it to. It's working.

Eventually, after a long time of playing, the game is over. I win.

When it's time for my second match, I tell myself that I have to play the same way as I did in the first. I'm playing Black this time, which means that my opponent is playing White and gets to move first, but I still keep my hands steady and tell myself *do not rush.*

TANI'S CHESS
TIP #7
Don't let your
opponent know
what you're
thinking.

I don't know how long the match takes. Maybe an hour and a half? Maybe two hours? I'm not counting. I'm deep thinking. I'm planning ahead and placing each piece just where I want it. When the match is over, I walk back to the team room and stand in the doorway.

I have to tell you something else

about the way that I play. No matter what I'm feeling in a match, I don't let anything show on my face, so I don't give my opponent any clue about what I'm thinking or feeling. So if I've just made the worst blunder ever or if I've suddenly seen a way to win, I don't change my expression at all. Even if I've got fireworks going off inside me, I still look completely serious on the outside. It's like I'm wearing a mask.

The weird thing is that when a game has finished, I can't take the mask off right away. I still look serious no matter if I've just won or been beaten.

So when I stand in the doorway and see Coach Shawn and Coach Russ and Mom and the others looking over at me, they can't tell from my face what just happened.

I like it.

They want me to tell them whether I won or lost, so I slowly hold out my arm with my hand bunched up tight in a fist. I poke my thumb out, then I point it right up in the air.

"Well done!" says Coach Russ.

"High five!" says Coach Shawn.

"Give me a hug!" says Mom.

I have to wait two hours before my final match of the day. So I do what I always do when I'm between games. I have a juice box and some candy and sit down with Coach Shawn to look through my notebook at the match I've just played.

"This is good," he says when we're done. "You're two and o, but let's not make a big deal of it. I want you to keep working on those openings, okay?"

I nod. There's a part of me that wants to spend my time *not* thinking about chess, but I know I need to keep my brain ready. I use a laptop to practice my favorite openings. As the computer program makes a move in response to my opening, I remind myself what to do, whatever move my opponent makes.

The time goes by quickly, and soon I'm back in the hall playing my last match of the day.

It's over really fast.

I'm standing back in the doorway to the team room with my arm held out. My thumb? It's sticking straight up.

When we're back at the house later that evening and have eaten some pizza, Mom tells me it's time for bed. But the coaches are all playing Blitz and saying funny things to each other, and the room is full of laughter and cheering.

"Please?" I say to her and Coach Shawn. "Can I just stay up for a while?"

Coach Shawn and Mom look at each other. I give both of them my biggest smile and say "Please!" a few more times.

"Okay," says Coach Shawn. "But just one game of Blitz and then you gotta go to bed straight after. Agreed?"

We play and he wins. Coach Shawn is so good, and he gets me with a trap that I don't see until the last minute. It's the first match I've lost all day, but I don't mind.

Before I say good night, he says, "Nice work, Tani. You're three and 0. If this was a one-day tournament, you'd have won."

I don't know what to say, so I just nod.

Coach Shawn has stopped talking, but I think he has something else to say. It's like he's being careful about making a move. He'll speak when he's ready.

"Tani," he says after a long wait. "You have a shot at actually winning this tournament now."

I *really* don't know what to say now. So I laugh. The laugh just kind of pops out.

"Get some sleep and be ready for a big day, okay?"

"Yes, Coach Shawn." I run up the stairs to bed. I hope that I can get to sleep.

CHAPTER 27

ROAR!

Because I'm eight years old, I play in the part of the tournament for kids in kindergarten through third grade. So I'm up against kids who are my age or nine years old, or they might be younger. Some of them, even the younger ones, are super good. I'm not the only player who starts the second day of the state championship on maximum points. There's a boy from a different school who is also coached by Coach Russ who has three points, like me, and I think there are some others who have won two games and drawn one, so they have two and a half points.

I try not to think about any of them.

When the second day starts, all I want to do is get into the team room, sit down in the same corner I sat in the day before, and get ready for the moment when Coach Shawn asks Zixi and me to lean in close and listen to him.

You never can tell what Coach Shawn is going to say when you're about to play a match. Sometimes he talks about strange things like being magically transported to France and being lost. Sometimes he has a gift, like the knights, and he talks about how we're warriors going into battle. But whatever he talks about, it always helps.

This time he has nothing in his hands. But his eyes are wide and smiling. "Do you know what you are? You're my lions, and I'm proud of you," he says. "And like all lions, you're made to go out onto that wide-open savanna and hunt. You've got speed and cunning and all the skills you need to track down your prey. So my question to you is this: Are you ready to go hunting?"

Zixi and I nod. I even let out a little roar.

I don't know how a lion would play chess, but all through my fourth match, I'm confident and calm and patient. All I need to do is stick to my plan and wait. Eventually, my opponent blunders, and I do what a good lion does: I pounce. The match is over pretty soon after that.

Everyone's happy that I won another match, but there are no cheers like yesterday. Four and o is good, but I want to do better. I want to go six and o.

To do that, I know what I need to do. After I've had my juice box and candy, I go back to the corner, take out my notebook, and get back to work.

If you want to be good at chess, there are some things that you have to be able to do. You have to be able to concentrate for a *looong* time on the board. You have to remember *all* the moves for your opening. You have to know how you're going to respond to the different traps your opponent is going to lay for you. All these things are part of deep thinking.

Coach Shawn is always telling us about deep thinking. He says things like, "You can't just find a *move*. You have to *have plans*." And he says, "This is what chess comes down to. Can you gather all the possible details of a position in your mind and then come up with a move that is either going to fix your weakness or increase your strength?"

He talks like this a lot at the chess program at PS 116 on Thursdays and at the Saturday morning club in Harlem. And whenever he talks about deep thinking, he sets us a challenge to help us get better and better at it.

Sometimes he puts a position up on the whiteboard and tells us to imagine that this is an actual match we're playing. Then he says, "I'm putting fifteen minutes on the clock. Find me three plans for how to get out of here."

Those fifteen minutes are tough. You have to look at the board, figure out your best move, and then imagine what your opponent might do. For each of their possible moves, you've got to have a plan. And when you're looking ahead like this, trying to think four or five moves into the future, you've got to always find the best possible move you could make. Coach Shawn calls them "candidate choices." And while you're working on these puzzles, he walks around saying things like, "Look for those candidate choices, people!" or "How's the king looking?" or "What's the pawn structure? What's your weakness? What needs to improve?"

Those fifteen minutes always go by fast. And when we're finished, Coach Shawn asks each of us to say what we think. We have to tell him which of our plans is the best one and why. Sometimes he even asks us what plan we'd use if our opponent was aggressive or defensive. It's hard work.

TANI'S CHESS
TIP #8
Think four or
five moves
ahead.

But it's how you learn to do deep thinking. And it's how you win.

I'm telling you this because something happens to me in my fifth game at the state championship, and it has to do with deep thinking.

I'm staring at the board. I'm staring *really* hard. I can't hear anything else that's going on around me, but I can *almost* hear Coach Shawn ask me to tell him about the pawns and the king and the weaknesses in my position and everything else that he is always getting me to say.

I work through each position. I look at each piece. I search for the best possible move that I could make, the ones that Coach Shawn calls the candidate choices. I'm looking further ahead in the match than I've ever looked and concentrating so hard that I don't know how long I've been sitting here.

And that's when I see it.

My opponent's king looks like it is well defended, but if I can just get him to move one of his pieces away, I have a feeling that his whole defense will collapse.

The trouble is, the only way I can see to get him to open up is to sacrifice one of my best pieces. It's just like a Paul Morphy move. It's a risk. It's the riskiest move I've ever made. It will either win me the match or lose it.

CHAPTER 28

DID I BLUNDER?

I know I said that when I've finished a match I look really serious, like I'm wearing a mask, but that's not always true.

When my fifth match is over and I'm walking out of the tournament hall with my opponent, I've got a big smile on my face. I'm even laughing.

My opponent is laughing too. "When I saw I could take your bishop I was like, what?"

"I know," I say. "You thought I'd blundered, right? You got my bishop, and all I got was a pawn."

"Yeah!"

We shake hands again, and he goes back to his team room. I don't even need to stick my thumb up to show people that I've won because they can tell from my face. But I stick it up anyway.

Mom is the first person to reach me. She pulls me in

super close in a massive hug and whispers a question in my ear. "Did you say thank you to God?"

I say my prayer out loud. "Thank You, God! Thank You, God! Thank You, God!"

"Well done," she says. "Now, I think Coach Shawn wants to talk to you."

I rush over to Coach Shawn. He's got the biggest smile I've ever seen on his face, and he's holding his hand up, ready for a high five.

"This is gonna hurt!" he says. And when he gives me the five it *really does hurt*. But I don't mind. I'm too busy laughing and hugging the other coaches.

It takes a while for everything to calm down and for Coach Shawn to ask for my notebook. Usually it's just Coach Shawn and me who review my game, but a lot of the other coaches are gathered around this time. They all read my notes in silence. But as they look and retrace my steps, they reach the point where I took the risk. And that's when they start talking.

"Why did you do that?" says Coach Shawn. "Sacrificing your bishop for a pawn like that—it's not what I would have expected."

"And there's another way," says Coach Russ. "A simpler one that could have gotten you to the same place in the end. Did you see it?"

"I know," I say. "But I wanted to sacrifice the bishop. I've seen someone do it before, and I wanted to try it."

Coach Shawn looks at me. I can tell he's surprised. "Where?"

"It was one of Paul Morphy's games."

I need to use the bathroom, so I leave the room for a few minutes. When I come back, the coaches are still standing around, but they're not looking at my notebook. They're looking at Coach Shawn's laptop.

On the screen is a chessboard. The pieces are arranged in the exact same way they were before I made my move and sacrificed my bishop.

"Uh, Tani," said Coach Russ. "Look at this."

He presses a button. A box opens on the screen that shows the best possible moves a player can make at this point. The moves are rated so you can tell which is the best one of all. I recognize it immediately.

It's the exact move that I made.

"You were right," Coach Russ says, pointing to the screen. "Sacrificing your bishop like that was the strongest move you could make."

Coach Shawn nods. "You're my lion all right. It's aggressive and unorthodox. It's pure Paul Morphy."

I'm super pleased about being five and o, but I don't have much time to think about it or to relax. The next game is an hour away, and I need to keep my mind in a place where I can do deep thinking.

I go to the corner where I've been hiding all through the tournament. Instead of looking at my notebook,

I borrow Coach Shawn's laptop and go through my favorite openings.

"That's good, Tani," says Coach Shawn. "Keep on putting your game in and memorize what it tells you. If you're making the number-one choice, that will be enough for you to win."

I do what he says, but inside my stomach, the elephant is jumping about. And my head is starting to feel hot as well.

Just when I'm wondering if I should have another juice box or visit the bathroom, I hear two of the coaches talking about how many points the other players have. I don't know which coach it is who says it, but the words rattle inside my head.

"Tani doesn't need to win. All Tani needs to do is draw."

I understand what he means. My opponent has won four matches and drawn one, so he only has four and a half points. I have the full five points. If we both draw, he'll have five and I'll have five and a half. But I've never played to draw before. I've always played to win.

All day I've known exactly what kind of moves I want to make. I've known what my strategy is, and I've known exactly how I want the board to look so I can win.

But playing to draw? I don't know how to do it. I'm confused and unsure, and then I feel even more nervous. This is the worst thing possible.

"It's time, Tani," says Coach Russ.

I know I should stand up to go, but I can't. For the first time in the entire state championship, I don't know if I'm ready.

CHAPTER 29

THE LAST MATCH

The hall is almost silent when I walk in for my last match. Every other time I've played, there have been lots of other people playing. But now that it's the end of the tournament, there are just two other matches taking place. I don't mind. The silence helps me think. But as I sit down and prepare to start, I feel like I need lots and lots of help.

It's not just that the coaches have told me to play for a draw. I'm distracted because, for the first time in the whole tournament, my opponent isn't a total stranger. I met him at summer camp. And I like him. He's fun.

But I don't want to lose.

I'm White, so I get to make the first move. All day I've been doing exactly what Coach Shawn has been telling me and memorizing the moves I want to make as well as the best moves that Black should make. That means I've got this map in my head of how the game should go. I know what a bad move looks like, and I know what a good move looks like.

The longer the match goes on, the more confident I am.

I've got the center of the board controlled. I'm using both my knights and both my bishops. I'm pleased with the way my pawns are looking. I'm calm and my hands are steady. I'm even remembering to place the pieces on the board slowly and carefully and to make sure they land right in the middle of the squares.

Coach Russ would be proud.

Then my opponent makes a mistake. It's not a big one, but it's definitely a mistake.

I don't just look at the board, I study it. I'm a lion again, searching the savanna. Or maybe I'm a knight on his horse looking out at the field of battle. Whatever I am, the longer I spend thinking about the next moves, the more sure I am that I'm going to win. It might take five more moves or maybe ten. But it's going to happen.

I make my next move then look at my opponent. I think he knows that it's going to be over soon too. He's staring at the board, holding in his breath. When he goes to move, his hand hovers over a piece for a few seconds, then he changes his mind and he chooses another piece. He's nervous.

Coach Shawn talks a lot about playing the player and not just the pieces. He often says that I need to watch my opponents for signs of nerves like this. "When they're worried," he says, "that's when you push hard."

It's time for my move. My thirteenth move of the match. In a couple of moves, I'm going to break into his pawns, so this move is all about building that attack.

I pick up the piece and set it down in an empty square. I'm confident. This is all going to be over soon.

TANI'S CHESS
TIP #9
Control the center of the board.

And then, just as I sit back in my seat and think about how he's going to respond, I feel sick inside.

I realize that I have blundered. My thirteenth move is not a little blunder either. It is not a small mistake. It is a supersized, giant blunder. The biggest one I've ever made. I've opened a door that will ruin everything. If my opponent looks hard enough and sees it, he'll probably be able to beat me in fewer than four moves.

My mouth goes dry.

I'm staring at the board, hoping that I'm wrong and that it's not a blunder after all. But the more I look, the more I know that I am lost. Totally lost. There's no way I can play my way out. It's over.

Unless . . .

Unless . . .

Could I get a draw? Could I somehow convince my opponent that he should accept a draw?

In chess you don't get to talk to your opponent. You can't say, "Hey, I don't really think that either of us is going to win this, so why don't we agree to draw?" All you can do is hold out your hand and say, "I offer a draw," and hope that your opponent agrees.

So that's what I do. I make myself sit up straight. I smile. I look him in the eye and pretend that I'm not at all worried as I stick out my hand. With my most confident voice, I say it. "I offer a draw."

He looks at me hard. Really hard. He's trying to read me, trying to work out why I'm offering a draw right now. If I were him, I wouldn't accept.

But I'm not him. I'm me. I keep my eyes on his and wave my hand to remind him that I want him to shake it. I don't want him to look at the board. If he does that, he might see that he can win.

He looks at me. I wait, my hand held out.

CHAPTER 30

DO YOU KNOW WHAT
YOU JUST DID?

My opponent opens his mouth, but no words come out right away. The silence stretches. My hand is getting tired.

Finally he speaks. "I accept," he says.

We shake hands. I pack up my notebook and pen, and then we go. Neither of us says anything. I think we're both tired.

As I walk back to the team room, I feel bad. I don't like that I've drawn, and I hate that I made such a bad blunder. So when I walk through the door, I'm not wearing a mask. I'm not pretending to look serious or sad. I really am feeling serious and sad.

Everyone's staring at me though, so I do what I always do. I hold my arm up and stick my thumb out sideways.

It takes a moment for them to realize that my thumb

isn't going to point up or down. It's just sticking there, pointing at the wall. Not a win. Not a loss.

Coach Shawn is the first one to come over to me. He's holding out his hands, like he wants me to give him the news myself.

"I drew," I say. The words sound heavy and flat.

But Coach Shawn is smiling, and he holds my shoulders with both hands. "You *drew*? Tani, do you know what you just did?"

"Yes. I drew." I know I should tell him about the blunder, but I don't want to. Not yet. So I say the only other thing I can think of. "It was a tough game, Coach Shawn."

He's not listening to me. Instead his eyes are wide like he's watching fireworks and his smile is as big as any smile I've ever seen. "But you drew, Tani! That means you won! You're the New York state champion!"

He tips back his head and shouts so loud that I think my ears might burst. "Tani drew! He's the champion!"

Coach Russ starts shouting, "Tani!" He rushes over to me, picks me up, and holds me so high in the air that I wonder if my head is about to hit the roof. "You're state champion," he says. "You won!"

For the first time since the match ended, I'm happy. But I'm still confused. "How can I be state champion when I came so close to losing? I made a really bad blunder, Coach Russ."

"But you *didn't* lose," he says. "Nobody scored more points than you."

Just then the door opens again, and one of the kids who belongs to another of Coach Russ's programs comes in. He's smiling and his coach runs over to him and starts shouting to the room that he's won his age group too.

Finally the excitement starts bursting inside me like fireworks. All the nerves and all the bad feelings about not winning suddenly disappear. Instead I feel great and excited and so happy. And to celebrate, I do some of my best-ever dancing, and all the coaches and adults in the room laugh so hard they nearly cry.

And then Mom comes over. She gives me a hug. A *big* hug. The *biggest* hug. When she's finished, she looks at me. She doesn't have to remind me to thank God for this miracle. I'm already saying it, over and over.

"Thank You, God! Thank You, God! Thank You, God!"

CHAPTER 31

THE TROPHY

After all the hugging and the high fives and the shouting in the team room, something even better happens.

I get my trophy.

Now, you know I like trophies, right? I've won a few, and I keep them neatly lined up on my dresser in my room at the Hotel. Most of them aren't very big, but the dresser top is getting a little crowded. In fact, the Hotel room feels like it's gotten smaller since we moved in. I guess it's because Austin and I are both growing. Sometimes I wish I could have more than just one small strip of floor between the beds. Sometimes I wonder what it would be like to have a room big enough to have a couch in it.

But back to the chess. When I see the trophy I've just won for becoming state champion, I can't believe it.

How to Play in a Chess Tournament

Contact your local chess club to find a nearby tournament. Ask whether you need to register before the day.

On the day of the tournament, bring chess pieces and a board, a chess clock (if you have one), and a book for recording your games. When you arrive, sign in and ask where and when you will be playing. This information is called "pairings." Your pairing will also tell you which board you will play at, who your opponent is, and whether you are White or Black.

When it's time for your first match, find your board and set up. Wait for the tournament director to tell you when to start, then shake your opponent's hand and have Black hit the clock. Now play!

When your game is over, shake your opponent's hand again. Then record your result on the pairings sheet. If you've lost, you won't have been eliminated, so don't leave! You can keep playing until the final round.

Record your result for each game. After the final round, stay to watch the awards. Tournaments often have prizes for players of different ratings, so you just might win something!

The trophy looks like one of the skyscrapers near the Hotel. It's almost as tall as me!

"Wow!" I say as I try to pick it up. I have to use *both hands*, and even then it's *sooooo* big and heavy. Everyone's laughing and cheering and taking photos with their phones.

"Tani," says Mom. "Look!" She's holding out her phone, and I can see Dad and Austin on the screen. Austin looks hot and sweaty and is dressed like he's just been playing basketball. Dad is wearing a suit. That's because he's not washing dishes any more. Dad's an Uber driver, which means he gets to dress smart every day. He likes it, and Austin likes playing basketball.

"Wow!" says Dad. "You won! You're state champion!"

"I know," I say. "I blundered and thought I was going to lose."

Austin shakes his head. "I knew you'd do it," he says. And then he says the nicest thing ever. "I'm proud of you, little brother."

I like playing lots of games in the same day, even if it means I have to work hard to concentrate for that long. But when the matches are over and it's time to go home, I'm so tired. My head starts to hurt, and I want to lie down and go to sleep.

It's a long drive back from Saratoga to New York City, and as soon as we climb inside the van, my eyes get heavy. I sit next to Mom and curl up against her. I can hear some of the coaches talking about chess, and I guess by the glow of their phone screens that some of them are playing matches, but I don't try and join in.

All I want to do is sleep and dream about trophies and tournaments and feeling happy enough to fly.

CHAPTER 32

CHANGING
THE WORLD

The next morning, everything is normal again. I get up for school. Miss Maria gives me a donut. Dad goes to work. Austin has early basketball practice. But as Mom walks me to school through the crowds, I try to figure out how I'm going to carry my trophy all the way if I'm allowed to bring it to school.

I like being back at school. I like seeing my friends, and I like my teachers. Some of them ask about the state championship, and I talk about it a little, but it's not a big deal. Besides, we're starting a new topic today that I'm looking forward to. We're going to learn about Martin Luther King Jr. and Malcolm X and Nelson Mandela. They all worked to stop people from treating black people worse than white people.

I like learning about these men. I like how Martin Luther King Jr. was kind of soft and Malcolm X was more aggressive and Nelson Mandela was so patient. They were all on the same path. Together they changed the world.

The only part of these lessons I don't like is learning that Martin Luther King Jr. was shot, and he died. Because of his death, a lot of other people took up his fight. But does that mean it was good for him to die? It can't have been good for his family. They must have been so sad.

Our teacher tells us a word I've not heard before. *Martyr.* It means someone who is killed because of what they believe. Martin Luther King Jr. was a martyr.

A few days after the tournament, I get asked to leave my class at school and go sit with a man from the *New York Times*, which is a famous newspaper here in the city. Mom, Dad, and Austin are there too. The reporter, Mr. Kristof, wants to talk to me about the state championship and how I won.

He's nice and he doesn't just want to talk about the tournament. He asks about Nigeria and the Hotel and Mom and Dad and what I like about living in America. There's a photographer with him too, which is strange. I'm glad when it's over because it's Thursday, and I don't want to be late for the chess program.

I don't think much more about Mr. Kristof and his questions until a couple of days later, when Dad comes to find me in my room in the Hotel.

He's holding his phone up against his chest and has got a very, very serious expression on his face. "Tanitoluwa," he says. For a moment I wonder whether I've done something wrong. "Do you want to see something great?" he asks.

"Um, yes please?"

Dad gives me his phone. There's a picture of me staring at a chessboard. Above it are the words, *This 8-Year-Old Chess Champion Will Make You Smile.*

I look back at Dad. He's not just smiling, he's laughing.

"What is it about?" I ask.

"You! Mr. Kristof has decided to tell the whole world about your story!"

I look back and try to read it. It's confusing at first, but when I get to the very end I read a line that I like a lot.

"'The US is a dream country,' his dad told me. 'Thank God I live in the greatest city in the world, which is New York, New York.'"

I look up at Dad. He's almost crying.

It's so weird reading Mr. Kristof's article on Dad's phone. But it's even weirder a couple of days later when Dad shows me that the same article is in the *actual newspaper*.

I like the picture of me staring at the chessboard, but I don't know about the one of me carrying my trophy as I cross the street with Mom and Austin. I look like I'm not very happy to have won, but at the time I was just thinking that I needed to concentrate because I didn't want to drop it.

But even reading about my own life or seeing a picture of myself in a newspaper is nothing compared to what happens next.

It all starts one afternoon when I get back from school. Mom and Dad are acting strange. They're looking at their phones a lot, laughing and saying things like "Wow!" and "God is good!"

"What's going on?" I ask.

They look at each other. Dad nods at Mom. "Coach Russ asked us if he could set up a fundraising page for us," she says.

"Why?"

"He thinks that people might want to give us some money so we can move from here and find a home of our own."

I have about two hundred questions. I want to know where we would move, when we would go there, and how far it would be from my school. I want to know who these people are and why Coach Russ thinks they will give us any money and whether we will have to pay it back. I want to know whether I'll still get my every-other-morning donut from Miss Maria and whether Austin and I will still have a room together. But I don't say any of this.

Mom and Dad are staring back at their phones, and their eyes are wide.

"What is it?" I ask.

It's Dad's turn to explain. "Coach Russ started the page, and an hour ago Mr. Kristof added the information to his article. People have already given thousands and thousands of dollars."

I still have all the same questions inside me, but I don't know what to say right now.

In the next few days, people give more and more. Mom and Dad talk about it, and I hear them using some *big* numbers. Ten thousand dollars. Twenty-five thousand dollars. Even fifty thousand dollars!

"Who's doing all this giving?" I ask. "Do they know us?"

Mom shakes her head. "They don't know much about us, and we don't know much about them. Some are from America, but people from all over the world are giving. Some have given big amounts of money, but most people are giving five or ten dollars each."

I try and do the sums in my head. I can't believe that there are so many people out there who would want to be generous to us.

In addition to the people who are giving money, other people send Dad messages about telling my story. He says there are TV stations, radio shows, and newspapers all over the world who want to interview us because they've heard about our story and how so many people are being generous. He gets messages from TV stations in Germany and Japan, Mexico, and China. The BBC in London wants to meet.

"And it's not just newspapers and TV shows," he says one day. "President Bill Clinton wants to see you!"

I've heard of him. "Why?" I say. "Did I do something wrong?"

Dad laughs. "No, Tani. He just wants to meet you. That's all."

The Canadian government sends us a beautiful chessboard. One of Dad's friends back home in Nigeria tells him that the main newspaper there printed the story and that some politicians talk about me. We also hear that in Morocco, they are going to make it a law that all school-children should be taught chess.

Someone even gives Dad a brand-new car! Now he doesn't have to rent a car to drive his Uber passengers.

But even *that* isn't the most amazing thing.

The best, most wonderful, most incredible, most awesome, most amazing thing that happens is this: someone gives us a place to live.

CHAPTER 33

BEING INTERVIEWED ON TV IS HARDER THAN PLAYING CHESS

I've never been inside a TV studio before, and as soon as I arrive at the NBC studio, I think it's strange. Part of the room has lights that are so bright they almost hurt your eyes, but the rest is dark like a cave. And there are people looking busy and running around and talking into headsets about things I don't understand. Someone tells me, "You just sit there on that couch and relax like you're sitting on the couch at home, okay?"

Should I tell them that we don't have a couch in our room at the Hotel? I decide not to and just say okay. But it isn't easy to relax. Not at all. I'm just glad that Coach Russ and Coach Shawn are with me.

I wonder if I should tell them that we don't have a TV in the Hotel. And because I don't get to watch it, I don't know who the people are who are sitting opposite me. They've all got big smiles, and people are helping them with their makeup—even the men—so I know they're the show hosts, but I don't know their names. They seem nice though.

Someone tells everyone to be quiet and it's like magic: the room goes silent, and the people on the other sofa freeze like statues. They're all staring at one of the TV cameras.

The woman sitting nearest me starts talking. She says that I'm "eight years old and well on the way to mastering the extremely difficult game of chess." I'm not sure about that. My rating is only 1562. Before I can call myself a master, I'll need to increase my score to something like 2200 or more. I don't say anything, though, because she stops talking and everything goes quiet while the picture of me with the trophy from the state championship appears on lots of TV screens in the studio.

Everybody watches a video about me. They'd filmed it at the Thursday chess club, and it says I'm a "chess champion capturing hearts." I'm not so sure about that either. All I know is that I didn't play very well when the cameras were pointing at me. I hope that nobody can tell from the video.

The screens go black when the video ends, and everyone is looking at me. The lights are super bright and

I want to look around, especially at the wall behind me. It's green, but on the TV screens that are all around the studio, there's no green wall, only pictures of me and my family. It's weird and makes it hard to concentrate.

Something tells me that I shouldn't get distracted and that I should try as hard as I can to look at the woman who is talking to me and listen to her question. I try. But it's even harder than playing chess.

"How did you feel when you won that championship?"

I say, "I felt surprised."

"Did you? You couldn't believe you got that good that fast?"

She's kind of wrong. I didn't feel surprised because of how quickly I'd improved. I felt surprised because I drew my last match and I'd come so close to losing it. But I don't think she wants me to explain all that, so I smile.

I'm happy that she starts asking Coach Russ and Coach Shawn about things. Being on TV is hard. But it can be good too. Coach Shawn is talking about my fifth game in the state cham-

TANI'S CHESS
TIP #10
Be willing to
sacrifice pieces.

pionship, when I sacrificed my bishop to win the match. He says, "In my mind, that was a master-level idea." I like that he says that. It makes me feel warm inside.

When the interview is nearly over, I'm thinking about leaving. It's not because I'm unhappy or I don't like being in the studio though. I mean, it's weird and hard not to get distracted, but being interviewed is okay, I guess.

I'm excited because there's something even better about to happen.

As soon as we leave the studio, we're going to visit our new home.

CHAPTER 34

HOME

I'm inside the elevator at our new apartment building. As we ride up to the third floor, the biggest laugh, the biggest smile, and the biggest shout *of my life* all swell inside me. And I'm not the only one. As soon as Dad opens the door to our new apartment and we all go inside, we start shouting. Not bad shouting but good shouting. Really good shouting.

"Wow! Wow! Wow!"

That's Dad.

"This is too much!"

That's Mom.

The rooms are all empty, and it looks *so big*. Austin and I are saying "yes!" and running from the kitchen to the living room to the hall to the first bedroom to the second bedroom, and then to the bathroom. Five whole rooms! We've both got the biggest grins. "This is *amazing*!" I say.

"I can't believe it!" says Austin.

When we get back into the living room, Mom and Dad and Coach Russ are on their knees. They're crying and praying at the same time.

"God, You're too much," prays Dad. "Wow! I know that You fed the five thousand and You parted the Red Sea, but this? It's too marvelous. Thank You!"

Mom joins in. "It doesn't matter if this place stays empty forever. Thank You, God!"

Austin and I kneel too. I say "Thank You, God" maybe a thousand times. The more I say it, the more the laughs and smiles and shouts grow from inside me.

There's so much excitement inside me that I can't keep still. So I stop kneeling and start rolling around on the floor. I can't control myself!

Then Mom and Dad and Austin and Coach Russ join in. We're all rolling around on the floor, laughing and saying "thank you!"

We're home.

CHAPTER 35

THIS IS WHAT
I THINK

A few months have passed since we were rolling around on the floor that day. The apartment isn't empty anymore. Lots of people have been generous, and we've got all the furniture we need.

Life is so much better.

The apartment has a great kitchen, so Mom doesn't have to go back to Pastor Philip's house three times a week to cook. That means we get to eat Nigerian food every day. I've got to tell you, if you start the morning with a bowl of jollof rice, you feel like *nothing* is going to go wrong.

The apartment is comfortable and big. When Austin and I play chess, we don't have to put the board on the floor between our beds. We've got a couch *and* a TV. We even have an AC for when it gets hot in the summer. The elevator is bigger and we've got our own key. There are so many things to be thankful for.

We've got a park too! I can't even remember if there was a place near the Hotel where Austin and I could go and play. But here at the apartment, there's a park with three basketball courts so close that I can run there in less than one minute.

Life is good.

Dad's driving Uber, and he's studying to become a real estate agent. Mom is working as a home aide, which means she helps people who are old or ill and who can't get out. Austin is doing super well at school. I've got more trophies in my room now, and there's space for even more—which might happen because my rating is getting higher. I'm really, truly, filled-to-the-top happy.

But there is something even better than our own kitchen and Mom's and Dad's jobs and parks and trophies. We've been able to use the money that people gave us to help others. Dad, Mom, and Coach Russ have set up the Tanitoluwa Adewumi Foundation, and it's going to help families who come to America and need help, just like we did. If they need clothes, the Foundation will buy them. If they need help with housing, the Foundation will help. And who knows, maybe one day one of the kids we help will become a chess champion. And maybe too, the

Foundation will grow and grow, and we really will have a skyscraper where other families who don't have a home can come and live with us.

There aren't so many people who want to interview me now, and I'm actually pleased about that. It's not easy to say what you think and explain yourself clearly to a stranger. But I've been doing a lot of thinking about everything that has happened to me and my family, and I've worked out a few things.

First. I want to be the youngest-ever chess grand master.

Right now the record is Sergey Karjakin. He was twelve years and seven months old when he became a grand master, so I have about four years to get there. It's going to be hard work, but I want to try. And if I get it? I'll set myself another goal and work toward that. Hard work pays off.

Second. More people should play chess.

It's fun, it makes you happy, and it helps you in life because you can learn how to think ahead and work out what might happen. And competition is really, really good, especially when you win.

Third. Winning feels good, but losing helps you learn.

I read a quote I really like: "Success is not permanent. Failure is not fatal. It is the courage to continue that counts." It means that if you win, that's good, but don't get all bigheaded. And if you lose, that's okay. Try again, work hard, learn from your mistakes. When you lose, you win—remember?

Fourth. It's really important to *never give up.*

The first five times I played chess at school, I lost. But I didn't give up. Mom, Dad, Coach Shawn, and others have all shown me that it's really important not to give up, even when things are tough and you feel like you're never going to win. And there have been so many times in a match when I've been losing, but I didn't give up. If you're down a piece it doesn't matter. Don't quit; stay in the game. If you're in the game, you still have a chance of winning.

Fifth. Everybody has a talent.

I'm not good at basketball. I'm never going to win a trophy there. But I want to keep on playing because getting better at something is always a good thing. A lot of people might have told you that you're not good at things. Maybe they're better than you, but that doesn't mean you should give up. Even if chess or basketball is not your talent, you've got to keep on going. Stick to the path that you know. Work hard. Keep on going.

And last, I believe in miracles.

Sometimes people ask me why I wear a cross. I wear it because it reminds me of Jesus and the fact that He's wonderful. He helps people become better. He loves us even though we make mistakes. And He makes miracles happen. Sometimes those miracles are big, like the ones in the Bible where someone gets healed or brought back to life. But often they're small, like Coach Russ letting me join the chess program for free or Miss Maria giving Austin or me a donut every day or Pastor Philip and the people at the Hotel all doing so much to help us.

Miracles are all around you. All you have to do is open your eyes and look.

I believe in miracles.

Do you?

SIDEBAR SOURCES

Chapter 1: Who Is an Immigrant?

Young, Patrick. "The Immigrants Among the Founding Fathers." Long Island Wins, July 3, 2014. https://longislandwins .com/news/national/the-immigrants-among-the-founding -fathers/.

Blakemore, Erin. "These Iconic Figures of American History Were All Immigrants." *Time*, November 12, 2015. https://time .com/4108606/history-american-immigrants/.

Sanchez, Gabriel H. "37 American Icons Who You Might Not Know Were Immigrants." BuzzFeed, February 2, 2017. https://www.buzzfeed.com/gabrielsanchez/american-icons -who-you-might-not-know-were-immigrants.

Tobin, Declan. "Immigration: the American Dream." American History for Kids. https://www.americanhistoryforkids.com /immigration-american-dream/.

Chapter 2: What Is Boko Haram?

"Who Are Nigeria's Boko Haram Islamist group?" BBC News,
November 24, 2016. https://www.bbc.com/news/world-
africa-13809501.

Counter Extremism Project. "Boko Haram." https://www
.counterextremism.com/threat/boko-haram.

Chapter 4: Chess around the World

Chessgames.com. "History of the World Chess Championship."
https://www.chessgames.com/wcc.html.

Chess-Site.com. "Chess Culture around the World." https://www
.chess-site.com/articles/chess-culture/.

Chapter 5: The Great Big Yoruba Family

"BBC Starts Igbo and Yoruba Services in Nigeria." BBC News,
February 19, 2018. https://www.bbc.com/news/world-
africa-43076923.

Sarkodie-Mensah, Kwasi. "Nigerian Americans." Countries and
Their Cultures. https://www.everyculture.com/multi/Le-Pa
/Nigerian-Americans.html.

Adewumi, Tani, with Kayode and Oluwatoyin Adewumi and Craig
Borlase. *My Name Is Tani . . . and I Believe in Miracles: The
Amazing True Story of One Boy's Journey from Refugee to
Chess Champion.* Nashville: Thomas Nelson, 2020.

Chapter 7: Profile: Nigeria

"Africa: Nigeria." In The World Factbook. CIA, 2019. https://www.
cia.gov/library/publications/the-world-factbook/geos
/print_ni.html.

Udo, Reuben Kenrick, Toyin O. Falola, Anthony Hamilton Millard Kirk-Greene, and J. F. Ade Ajayi. "Nigeria." In Encyclopaedia Britannica Online. https://www.britannica.com/place/Nigeria.

World Population Review. "Abuja Population 2019." May 12, 2019. http://worldpopulationreview.com/world-cities/abuja-population.

Favre, Lauren. "10 Interesting Facts about Nigeria." *U.S. News*, July 2, 2019. https://www.usnews.com/news/best-countries/articles/2019-07-02/10-interesting-facts-about-nigeria

Answers Africa. "10 Fun, Interesting Facts about Nigeria." https://answersafrica.com/facts-about-nigeria.html.

Science Kids. "Nigeria Facts for Kids." Country Facts. http://www.sciencekids.co.nz/sciencefacts/countries/nigeria.html.

Chapter 12: How to Play Chess

Chess.com. "How to Play Chess: Rules + 7 Steps to Begin." April 25, 2019. https://www.chess.com/learn-how-to-play-chess.

ChessU. "Chess Setup and Rules for Kids & Beginners." 2012. http://www.chesscoachonline.com/chess-articles/chess-rules.

Chess Corner. "Learn to Play Chess." 2019. http://www.chesscorner.com/tutorial/learn.htm.

Chapter 15: Profile: New York City

A., Alex. "Founded in 1905, Lombardi's Is the First Pizzeria in the United States." *Vintage News*, September 20, 2016. https://www.thevintagenews.com/2016/09/20/priority-birthplace-pizza-america-founded-1905-lombardis-first-pizzeria-united-states-2.

McGinniss, Paul. "Profile: New York City, New York." Great American Country. https://www.greatamericancountry.com/places/local-life/profile-new-york-city-new-york.

Lankevich, George. "New York City." In Encyclopaedia Britannica
 Online. https://www.britannica.com/place/New-York-City.
Amaya, Nigel. "How Many Languages Are Spoken in NYC?"
 WorldAtlas, November 9, 2018. https://www.worldatlas.com
 /articles/how-many-languages-are-spoken-in-nyc.html.
City of New York. "Population—New York City Population."
 Department of City Planning. https://www1.nyc.gov/site
 /planning/planning-level/nyc-population/population-facts.page.
Oldest.org. "8 Oldest Pizzerias in New York." Food. http://www
 .oldest.org/food/pizzerias-in-new-york/.

Chapter 31: How to Play in a Chess Tournament

Scimia, Edward. "Playing in Your First Chess Tournament." The
 Spruce Crafts, January 13, 2019. https://www.thesprucecrafts
 .com/your-first-chess-tournament-611569.
A Parent's Guide to Scholastic Chess Tournaments. Georgia Chess
 Association. http://www.georgiachess.org/resources/Documents
 /A%20Parent's%20Guide%20to%20Scholastic%20Chess%20
 Tournaments.pdf

Tani Adewumi is the Nigerian-born boy who won the 2019 New York State Chess Championship after playing the game for only a year. Tani and his family's story begins amidst Boko Haram's reign of terror in their native country of Nigeria and takes them to a New York City homeless shelter, where they waited to be granted religious asylum. Tani's father, who came from a royal Nigerian family, became a dishwasher and Uber driver to support his family. Tani's mother, whose family owned the largest printing press in Nigeria and who had been working at a bank for over a decade, trained to become a home aide. So, when Tani asked to join the chess program at his elementary school, which required a fee, it seemed unlikely. His mother wrote to the coach, who offered Tani a scholarship. Miracles led Tani and his family to New York. As Tani's father puts it, "There are many times in my life where I thought, *this must be the miracle*, and yet I did not know that the miracle had not yet begun."